Understanding Non·Christian Religions

BOOKS BY JOSH MCDOWELL

Reasons Skeptics Should Consider Christianity

Prophecy: Fact or Fiction

More Than a Carpenter

Evidence That Demands a Verdict

Evidence Growth Guide: The Uniqueness of Christianity

More Evidence That Demands a Verdict

The Resurrection Factor

The Resurrection Factor Growth Guide

Answers to Tough Questions

Givers, Takers and Other Kinds of Lovers

Handbook of Today's Religions — Understanding the Cults

Handbook of Today's Religions — Understanding the Occult

Handbook of Today's Religions — Understanding
Non-Christian Religions

Josh McDowell & Don Stewart

◇ HANDBOOK OF ◇ TODAY'S RELIGIONS

Understanding Non·Christian Religions

CAMPUS CRUSADE FOR CHRIST
Published by
HERE'S LIFE PUBLISHERS, INC.
San Bernardino, California 92402

HANDBOOK OF TODAY'S RELIGIONS
Understanding Non-Christian Religions
by Josh McDowell
and Don Stewart

Library of Congress Catalog Card 81-86543
ISBN 0-86605-092-2
HLP Product No. 402834
© Copyright 1982 by Campus Crusade for Christ, Inc.

Printed in the United States of America

FOR MORE INFORMATION, WRITE:

L. I. F. E. — P. O. Box A399, Sydney South 2000, Australia
Campus Crusade for Christ of Canada — Box 368, Abbottsford, B. C., V25 4N9, Canada
Campus Crusade for Christ — 103 Friar Street, Reading RGI IEP, Berkshire, England
Campus Crusade for Christ — 28 Westmoreland St., Dublin 2, Ireland
Lay Institute for Evangelism — P. O. Box 8786, Auckland 3, New Zealand
Life Ministry — P. O. Box / Bus 91015, Auckland Park 2006, Republic of So. Africa
Campus Crusade for Christ, Int'l. — Arrowhead Springs, San Bernardino, CA 92414, U.S.A.

"Beloved, believe not every spirit, but try the spirits whether they are of God, because many false prophets are gone out into the world" (1 John 4:1 KJV).

Table of Contents

Introduction   9

Chapter 1 Hinduism   17

         2 Jainism   35

         3 Buddhism   47

               Nichiren Shoshu Buddhism   63

               Zen Buddhism   66

         4 Confucianism   77

         5 Taoism   97

         6 Shintoism   111

         7 Zoroastrianism   121

         8 Judaism   131

         9 Islam   149

        10 Sikhism   181

Appendix:

    A Christian Approach to Comparative Religions   189

For Further Reading   203

The Four Laws   209

Introduction

There are more than four billion people living in the world today, most of whom are associated with one or another of the world's major religions. Although most people have some sort of religious affiliation, they are woefully ignorant as to the basic beliefs of their own religion. Not only do most people have a shallow understanding of their own faith, but most have very little knowledge of any of the other world religions.

With the advance of modern technology, the world has shrunk to the point that we would do well to know and understand what our neighbors believe. This book is an effort to fill this information gap by giving the reader a working knowledge of the great religions of the world. No attempt has been made to treat each religion in an exhaustive manner, but rather to present each one's basic beliefs and key concepts.

We have evaluated each religion briefly in light of the beliefs and teachings of Christianity. A more extensive treatment of Christian belief and truth can be found in the lengthy section on Christian doctrine in volume *one* of this series, *Understanding the Cults*. An annotated reading list at the end of this volume will guide you in further study.

What Is Religion?

The term religion has many definitions. None is agreed upon by everyone, but certain common aspects and implications of religion can be observed. We define religion as that aspect of one's experience in which he attempts to live harmoniously with the power or powers he believes are controlling the world.

John B. Noss relates some of the implications of religious belief:

> All religions imply in one way or another that man does not, and cannot, stand alone, that he is vitally related with and even dependent on powers in nature and society external to himself. Dimly or clearly, he knows that he is not an independent center of force capable of standing apart from the world.... Religions, as a general rule, relate men closely with the power or powers at work in nature and society.... Most men from primitives in the jungle to members of societies far advanced in technology and intercultural relationships, do not think that men are all that matters (John B. Noss, *Man's Religions*, New York: MacMillan Company, 1969, p. 2).

The derivation of the word *religion* suggests several possible readings, as Herbert Stroup reveals:

> The English word "religion" derives from the Latin *religio*. Even so, there is no clear agreement as to the meaning of the word. Servius and others, for example, held that it came from the root "lig-", which means "to bind." Religion in this sense would signify a relationship—the binding relationship between man and God. Yet Cicero believed that the word was derived from the root "leg-", which means "to take up, gather, count, or observe." The meaning here suggests the observation of the signs of divine communication. In later times, both meanings were accepted by Augustine, for example, and today there seems to be little if any question regarding the propriety of either derivation (Herbert Stroup, *Four Religions of Asia*, New York: Harper & Row, 1968, p. 6).

Religion Is Universal

Religion is a universal phenomenon. Wherever man lives he is found giving some recognition to a power or powers beyond himself. Joseph Gaer comments appropriately:

> As far as we can determine, religion has existed in every society, from the most primitive to the most culturally advanced. The more keys modern science finds with which to open the locked doors of the past, and the more we learn about the early days of man on earth, the more evidence there

is that all these societies in the past had one thing in common – some form of religion.

Some of these early men were more advanced than others. And while some progressed continually in an upward trend, others remained stationary after reaching a certain stage of development. Still others retrogressed. Yet all of these early men, whatever their rate of development or whatever their differences, left behind unmistakable signs that they had each practiced a religion of their own (Joseph Gaer, *What the Great Religions Believe*, New York: Dodd, Mead, and Company, 1963, p. 16).

Religion is not only universal, it is also one of the features separating man from the animal world. "Religion is one of the things which distinguishes man from the other animals. Apes and dolphins, as far as we know, have no religions, but no group of human beings has ever been discovered which did not have religious beliefs" (Richard Cavendish, *The Great Religions*, New York: Arco Publishing, Inc., 1980, p. 2).

Religion Meets Needs

The function of religion has an indispensable aspect in all human life. It is those higher beliefs or ultimate concerns which keep us all going. Robert E. Hume comments on the function of religion:

> Religion gives to a person what he can obtain from no other source – a confidence in the outcome of life's struggles through a personal connection with the superior Power or powers in the world. Every religion does many things for the religious individual and also usually for society. For example, it assists in providing the individual with added power and satisfaction; it helps him to bear the troubles of life uncomplainingly; it offers a solution of the problem of evil; it improves the quality of this present life; it offers the hope of a better life in the future; it outlines an ideal society; it sets a working plan of salvation.
>
> The distinguishing function of religion, in contrast with that of philosophy or ethics, or any of the idealizing or cultural activities, is to give to a human being the supreme satisfaction of his life through a vital relationship with what he recognizes as the superhuman Power, or powers, in the world (Robert E. Hume, *The World's Living Religions*, New York: Charles Scribner's Sons, rev. ed., 1959, pp. 3, 4).

The Practice of Religion

The practice of religion is as varied as the religions themselves. Marcus Bach writes:

> Religion means different things to different men. To the primitive it means offering his animal sacrifices, and to the aborigine it means mutilating his body. It may be expressed in baptismal ceremonies for the dead and in spiritual exercises for the living. It is man attempting to prove the mystery of life and probing the riddle that death is but the lighted passage to another world.
>
> Religion is the priest at his altar and the minister in his pulpit. It is the neophyte first learning the concepts of his faith and the penitent in his confession. It is a cross, a book, a candle, a hope, a song. It is work and play and even ceremonies for war and peace (Marcus Bach, *Major Religions of the World*, Nashville: Abingdon Press, 1977, p. 12).

All Religions Are Not the Same

A common misconception is that all religions are basically saying the same thing or that all religious "paths" eventually reach the same summit — God.

An advocate of this view, Bhagavan Das, writes the following in the introduction to one of his books:

> Throughout history men have followed the religious faith of their own culture, and the majority have accepted their own faith as the only embodiment of truth. Yet in every religion there have been wise men holding the candle of light by which wisdom can be seen. This book shows how false are the barriers which have been erected between the different religions. The author has compiled passages from the scriptures of the world's eleven major living religions to show the similarity of their principles. Excerpts from the holy writings of the Christians, Jews, Hindus, Buddhists, Muslims, as well as other religions of India, Persia, China and Japan — all translated into English — have been arranged in parallel form to illustrate their unity. The author demonstrates how each great religion is another statement of the same timeless truths (Bhagavan Das, *The Essential Unity of All Religions*, Wheaton, IL: The Theosophical Publishing House, 1966).

Das goes on to advocate that this universal religion must be taught to all mankind:

> *The Universal Religion — That in which there may be*

Universal Agreement. We have heard of the Three R's long enough. This fourth R, of genuine Universal Religion, is more important than them all, and ought to be added to them everywhere, in every school and college *(Ibid.*, p. 54).

It simply is not true that all religions are basically the same. Although similar teachings do occur in more than one religion, the differences between them are as marked as night and day. Richard Cavendish illustrates the point in this manner:

> For example, the attitudes of the major religions to salvation and the purpose of life are quite different. In Judaism, Christianity and Islam, salvation means the survival of the individual personality in a happy existence in heaven after death. In Hinduism and Buddhism, on the other hand, salvation may mean the opposite, not the survival but the obliteration of the individual personality.
>
> Christianity believes in a divine Saviour, who came into the world to rescue man, but Judaism and Islam strongly disapprove of this belief as a gross breach of monotheism, the belief in a single god. Christianity, Judaism and Islam all agree, however, that human beings live only once on the earth and so have only one chance to make sure of a happy afterlife.
>
> Life on earth is therefore a profoundly serious affair and it is essential to get it right. But in Hinduism and Buddhism human beings live over and over again on the earth, born and reborn again indefinitely, and there is literally all the time in the world to get things right. It is hardly surprising, consequently, that Hinduism and Buddhism are far more tolerant than Judaism, Christianity and Islam (Richard Cavendish, *op. cit.*, p. 8).

The following chart dispels the idea that all religions are the same. Not only do they have a diversity of sacred books, but they also worship a diversity of deities.

RELIGION	DATE FOUNDED		FOUNDER	DEITY*	SACRED BOOKS
Judaism	ca	1800 B.C.	Abraham	Yahweh	Law, Prophets and Writing
Hinduism	ca	1500 B.C.	None	Brahman and many others	Vedas
Shinto	ca	660 B.C.	None known	Nature-gods	Ko-ji-ki and Nihon-gi
Zoroastrianism		660 B.C.	Zoroaster	Ahura Mazda	Avesta
Taoism		604 B.C.	Lao-tze	The Tao	Tao Te Ching
Jainism		599 B.C.	Mahavira	Originally none; now Mahavira	Angas
Buddhism		560 B.C.	Guatama Buddha	Originally none; now Buddha	Tripitaka
Confucianism		551 B.C.	Confucius	Heaven	The Classics
Christianity	ca	4 B.C.	Jesus Christ	Yahweh	Bible (Old and New Testaments)
Islam		A.D. 570	Mohammed	Allah	Koran
Sikhism		A.D. 1469	Nanak	True Name	Granth Sahib

* *Deity* is used loosely here. It may mean a traditional concept of God (as in Judaism); an impersonal supreme Power (as in Hinduism); or a founder, reverence for whom has developed into devotion or even worship (as in Buddhism).

Introduction Bibliography

Bach, Marcus, *Major Religions of the World*, Nashville: Abingdon Press, 1977.

Cavendish, Richard, *The Great Religions*, New York: Arco Publishing, Inc., 1980.

Das, Bhagavan, *The Essential Unity of All Religions*, Wheaton, IL: Theosophical Publishing House, 1966.

Gaer, Joseph, *What the Great Religions Believe*, New York: Dodd, Mead, and Company, 1963.

Hume, Robert E., *The World's Living Religions*, New York: Charles Scribner's Sons, rev. ed., 1959.

Noss, John B., *Man's Religions*, New York: MacMillan Company, 1969.

Stroup, Herbert, *Four Religions of Asia*, New York: Harper and Row, 1968.

Hinduism

Hinduism is not only one of the oldest of all religious systems, it is also one of the most complex. During its history Hinduism has spawned a variety of sects holding diverse beliefs; therefore, it is difficult to get an accurate picture of Hinduism without considering a vast array of history and commentary. John B. Noss states:

> It is not one religion, but rather a family of religions.... Hinduism is fluid and changing....Hinduism is the whole complex of beliefs and institutions that have appeared from the time when their ancient (and most sacred) scriptures, the vedas, were composed until now....Hindus have an extraordinarily wide selection of beliefs and practices to choose from: they can (to use Western terms) be pantheists, polytheists, monotheists, agnostics, or even atheists (John B. Noss, *Man's Religions*, New York: MacMillan Company, 1969, p. 88).

Joseph Gaer lists some of the complexities of Hinduism:

> Just as the attributes of the Hindu Triad multiplied until there were millions of them, and the castes divided and subdivided from the original four to a very large number, so also has this extremely old religion given rise to many sects.
>
> There are sects who worship Vishnu as the god of space and time.
>
> There are sects who worship Shiva (or Lord Siva) as a god of song and healing.
>
> There are sects who worship Durga, the Divine Mother (goddess of motherhood).

And there are many others. But all the various sects believe in:

Brahman, the eternal Trimutri, or Three-in-One God: *Brahma*, the Creator; *Vishnu*, the Preserver; and *Shiva*, the Destroyer;

Submission to Fate, since man is not outside, but part of Brahman;

The *Caste System*, determined by the Laws of Manu;

The *Law of Karma*, that from good must come good, and from evil must come evil;

Reincarnation, as a chain of rebirths in which each soul, through virtuous living, can rise to a higher state;

Nirvana, the final stage reached upon the emancipation of the soul from the chain of rebirths;

Yogas, the disciplines which enable the individual to control the body and the emotions; and

Dharma, the Law of Moral Order, which each individual must find and follow to reach nirvana (Joseph Gaer, *What the Great Religions Believe*, New York: Dodd, Mead, and Company, 1963, p. 35).

Because of its many complexities, Hinduism seemingly is impossible to summarize, as John Bowker observes:

To summarize the thought of any religion is difficult, but in the case of Hinduism it is impossible. It is the essence of Hinduism that there are many different ways of looking at a single object, none of which will give the whole view, but each of which is entirely valid in its own right. A statue may be viewed from many angles. Each aspect helps to convey what the statue is like, but no single aspect is able to comprehend the statue as a whole, still less does the act of viewing it from one particular angle or another constitute "the statue itself" (John Bowker, *Problems of Suffering in Religions of the World*, London: Cambridge University Press, 1970, p. 193).

Hinduism as a Universal Religion

Hinduism is tolerant of other religions because Hindus see a sameness in all of them:

The truth, which is the kernel of every religion, is one and the same; doctrines, however, differ considerably since they are the applications of the truth to the human situation... Rites, ceremonies, systems and dogmas lead beyond themselves to a region of utter clarity and so have only relative truth...Every work, every concept is a pointer which points beyond itself. The sign should not be mistaken for the thing signified. The sign-post is not the destination (S. Radhakrishnan, *East and West, The End of Their Separation*, New York: Alen & Uniwin, Humanities Press, 1954, p. 164).

Different religious leaders have belonged to different schools, and most Hindus are rather proud of the fact that there have not been any violent conflicts or persecution, thanks to mutual tolerance. This is a field where no one theory can claim to explain all the mysteries, and tolerance may well be the path to wisdom rather than that to confusion (K. M. Sen, *Hinduism*, London: Gannon Publ., 1963, pp. 84 ff).

Hindu Scriptures

The Hindu scriptures, written over a period of 2,000 years (1400 B.C.-500 A.D.) are voluminous. They reflect the practices and beliefs which arose during the different long periods of Hindu history. Bruce Nichols explains:

The Hindu scriptures are divided into two classes — *sruti* and *smriti*. Sruti, or "what is heard," refers to the eternal truths of religion which the *rishis* or seers saw or heard. They are independent of any god or man to whom they are communicated. They are the primary and final authority of religious truth. Using the analogy of the reflection of an image in a mirror or on the surface of a lake, the intellect of the ancient *rishis* was so pure and calm that it perfectly reflected the entirety of eternal truth. Their disciples recorded this truth and the record of it is known as the *vedas*. Smriti, or "what is remembered," possess a secondary authority, deriving their authority from the *sruti* whose principles they seek to expand. As recollections they contain all the sacred texts other than the *vedas*. These are generally understood to include the law books, the two great epics, the *Ramayana* and the *Mahabharata*, and the *Puranas*, which are largely collections of myths, stories, legends and chronicles of great events. Also included are the *aqamas*, which are theological treatises and manuals of worship, and the *sultras*, or aphorisms, of the six systems of philosophy. There is also a vast treasury of vernacular literature largely of a *bhakti* or devotional type, which continues to inspire the masses of religious Hindus and which different sects accept as *smriti* (Bruce Nichols in *The World's Religions*, Sir Norman Anderson, ed., Grand Rapids: Wm. B. Eerdmans Publishing Company, 1976, pp. 137, 138).

The Vedas

The word *veda* literally means wisdom or knowledge. It is the term applied to the oldest of the Hindu scriptures, originally transmitted orally and then subsequently preserved in written form. The vedas contain hymns, prayers and ritual texts composed over a period of one thousand years, beginning about 1400 B.C.

The term vedas (plural) refers to the entire collection of these wisdom books, also known as the *samhitas*, which include the *rig-veda*, the *sama-veda*, the *yajur-veda* and the *athara-veda*. Each of these texts consists of three parts: (1) the *mantras*, hymns of praise to the gods; (2) the *brahmanas*, a guide for practicing ritual rights, and (3) the *upanishads*, the most important part of which deals with teachings on religious truth or doctrine.

The *samhitas* are the basis of vedic Hinduism, the most significant of the group being the *rig-veda*. This collection of hymns, originally composed in Sanskrit, praises the various Hindu deities, including Indra, Soma, Varuna and Mitra.

The *yajur-veda* consists of a collection of mantras borrowed from the rig-veda and applied to specific ritual situations carried out by the executive priest and his assistants.

The *sama-veda* in the same manner borrows mantras from the rig-veda. These hymns are chanted.

The *athara-veda* consists of magical spells and incantations carried out by the priests.

The Upanishads

The *upanishads* are a collection of speculative treatises. They were composed during the period 800 to 600 B.C., and 108 of them are still in existence. The word *upanishad* conveys the idea of secret teaching. Its treatises mark a definite change in emphasis from the sacrificial hymns and magic formulas in the vedas to the mystical ideas about man and the universe, specifically the eternal Brahman, which is the basis of all reality, and the *atman*, which is the self or the soul. The upanishads reportedly had an influence upon Gautama Buddha, the founder of Buddhism, as can be observed in some basic similarities between the upanishads and the teachings of Mahayana Buddhism.

Ramayana

The *Ramayana* is one of the two major epic tales of India, the other being the *Mahabharatha*. Authorship is ascribed to the sage-poet Valmiki. The work consists of 24,000 couplets based upon the life of Rama, a righteous king who was supposedly an incarnation of the god Vishnu.

Although the story has some basis in fact, much of it is layered folklore added throughout the centuries. Besides Valmiki, other poets and writers have contributed to the complexities of the story. Edward Rice gives a brief synopsis of the account:

> Rama, a warrior and wanderer in the great tradition (one might equate him to Gilgamesh and Odysseus), is faced with a series of challenges and tests, some of which involve battles with other kings, or with demons; his wife Sita is kidnaped by a demon king and carried off in an air chariot to Ceylon; his chastity and faithfulness are tested; great battles ensue; the ending is a happy one, with Rama restored to the throne of Ayodha, and eventually he and Sīta, after more trials, are united, not on earth but in the celestial abodes.
>
> By the time the innovators have finished the story, Rama and Sita are not only avatars of Vishnu but also exemplars of all the mundane and spiritual qualities with which the cosmos is endowed. The work has special interest to historians and ethnologists, for many elements depict the social conditions of the peninsula during that period. It is involved in the conflict of the Aryans with the aborigines and the Aryanization of the latter; the monkeys and bears who were allies of Rama were actually aborigines who bore animal names as totems, as they still do today (Edward Rice, *Eastern Definitions*, Garden City, NJ: Doubleday, 1980, p. 296).

The Mahabharata

The *Mahabharata* is the second epic, an immense story of the deeds of Aryan clans. It consists of some 100,000 verses and was composed over an 800-year period beginning about 400 years B.C. Contained within this work is a great classic, the *Bhagavad Gita*, or the "Song of the Blessed Lord."

Bhagavad Gita

This work is not only the most sacred book of the Hindus, it is also the best known and most read of all Indian works in the entire world, despite the fact it was added late to the Mahabharata, sometime in the first century A.D. The story, in short, consists of a dialogue between Krishna, the eighth Avatar of Vishnu, and the warrior Arjuna, who is about to fight his cousins. The question Arjuna asks Krishna is: How can he kill his blood relatives?

> Krishna! as I behold, come here to shed
> Their common blood, yon concourse of our kin,
> My members fail, my tongue dries in my mouth,
> A shudder thrills my body, and my hair
> Bristles with horror; hardly may I stand.
>   ...What rich spoils
> Could profit; what rule recompense; what span
> Of life seem sweet, bought with such blood?
> Seeing that these stand here, ready to die,
> For whose sake life was fair, and pleasure pleased,
> And power grew precious: — grandsires, sires, and sons,
> Brothers, and fathers-in-law, and sons-in-law,
> Elders and friends!
> So speaking, in the face of those two hosts,
> Arjuna sank upon his chariot-seat,
> And let fall bow and arrows, sick at heart (*The Bhagavad Gita*, 1:28-47).

The story revolves around man's duty, which if carried out will bring nothing but sorrow. The significance this story has on Hindu belief is its endorsement of bhakti, or devotion to a particular god, as a means of salvation, since Arjuna decides to put his devotion to Vishnu above his own personal desires. The Gita ends with Arjuna devoted to Vishnu and ready to kill his relatives in battle.

This poem has inspired millions of Hindus who have identified Arjuna's dilemma with their own situation. The poem offers hope, through the way of devotion, to all people no matter what their caste or sex. The poor and downtrodden, who could not achieve salvation through the way of works or the way of knowledge, can now achieve it through the way of devotion.

These two epic stories, the Ramayana and the

Mahabharata, depict characters who have become ideals for the people of India in terms of moral and social behavior.

The Puranas

The Puranas are a very important source for the understanding of Hinduism. They include legends of gods, goddesses, demons and ancestors. They describe pilgrimages and rituals to demonstrate the importance of bhakti, caste and dharma. This collection of myths and legends, in which the heroes display all the desirable virtues, has made a significant contribution to the formation of Hindu moral codes.

Hindu Teachings (Doctrine)

To achieve a proper understanding of the world view held by the Hindus, it is necessary to present some of the basic concepts they hold to be true.

Brahman

Brahman, the ultimate reality for the Hindu, is a term difficult if not impossible to define completely, for its meaning has changed over a period of time. Edward Rice explains it in the following manner:

> The Supreme Reality conceived of as one and undifferentiated, static and dynamic, yet above all definitions; the ultimate principle underlying the world, ultimate reality: "Without cause and without effect, without anything inside or outside," according to the sage Yajñavalkya. "Brahman is he whom speech cannot express, and from whom the mind, unable to reach him, comes away baffled," states the *Taittinya Upanishad*. Brahman is now of interest more as a philosophic concept of past ages than as an active principle — to be meditated upon, but not adored or worshiped (*Ibid*, p. 71).

The enigmatic concept of Brahman is illustrated in this famous passage from the Bhagavad-Gita:

> "Place this salt in water and come to me tomorrow morning." Svetaketu did as he was commanded, and in the morning his father said to him: "Bring me the salt you put into the water last night."

Svetaketu looked into the water, but could not find it, for it had dissolved.

His father then said: "Taste the water from this side. How is it?"

"It is salt."

"Taste it from the middle. How is it?"

"It is salt."

"Taste it from that side. How is it?"

"It is salt."

"Look for the salt again, and come again to me."

The son did so, saying: "I cannot see the salt. I only see water."

His father then said: "In the same way, O my son, you cannot see the spirit. But in truth he is there. An invisible and subtle essence is the Spirit of the whole universe. That is Reality. That is Truth. THOU ARE THAT!"

Moksha

Moksha, also known as *mukti*, is the Hindu term used for the liberation of the soul from the wheel of karma. For the Hindu, the chief aim of his existence is to be freed from *samsara* (the binding life cycle) and the wheel of karma with its endless cycle of births, deaths and rebirths. When one achieves this liberation, he enters into a state of fullness or completion. This state can be attained through death or preferably while one is still living.

Moksha can be achieved through three paths: (1) knowledge, or *jnana*; (2) devotion, or *bhakti*, or (3) ritual works, or *karma*. One who achieves moksha before death is known as jivanmukta.

Atman

Atman is another Hindu term which is difficult to define. It refers to the soul or true self, the part of each living thing that is eternal. The *Taittiriya Upanishad* says atman is "that from which speech, along with the mind, turns away—not able to comprehend." Oftentimes, it is used synonymously with Brahman, the universal soul, seeking mystical union together, or moksha.

Maya

A central concept in Hindu thought is that of *maya*. Huston Smith expands upon the meaning of this key concept as follows:

This word is often translated "illusion," but this is misleading. For one thing it suggests that the world need not be taken seriously. This the Hindu would deny, pointing out that as long as it appears real and demanding to us we must accept it as such. Moreover, it does have a kind of qualified reality; reality on a provisional level.

Were we to be asked if dreams are real, our answer would have to be qualified. They are real in the sense that we have them, but they are not real in the sense that the things they depict necessarily exist in their own right. Strictly speaking a dream is a psychological construct, something created by the mind out of its particular state. When the Hindus say the world is maya, this too, is what they mean. Given the human mind in its normal condition, the world appears as we see it. But we have no right to infer from this that reality is in itself the way it so appears.

A child seeing a motion picture for the first time will assume that the objects he sees—lions, kings, canyons—are objectively before him; he does not suspect that they are being projected from a booth in the rear of the theater. It is the same with us; we assume the world we see to be in itself as we see it whereas in actuality it is a correlate of the particular psycho-physical condition our minds are currently in. (Huston Smith, *The Religions of Man*, New York: Harper and Row, 1958, pp. 82, 83.)

Karma

The word *karma* literally means *action* and has reference to a person's actions and the consequences thereof. In Hinduism, one's present state of existence is determined by his performance in previous lifetimes. The law of karma is the law of moral consequence, or the effect of any action upon the performer in a past, a present or even a future existence. As one performs righteous acts, he moves towards liberation from the cycle of successive births and deaths.

Contrariwise, if one's deeds are evil, he will move further from liberation. The determining factor is one's karma. The cycle of births, deaths and rebirths could be endless. The goal of the Hindu is to achieve enough good karma to remove himself from the cycle of rebirths and achieve eternal bliss.

Samsara

Samsara refers to transmigration or rebirth. It is the

passing through a succession of lives based upon the direct reward or penalty of one's karma. This continuous chain consists of suffering from the results of acts of ignorance or sin in past lives. During each successive rebirth, the soul, which the Hindus consider to be eternal, moves from one body to another and carries with it the karma from its previous existence.

The rebirth may be to a higher form; i.e., a member of a higher caste or god, or down the social ladder to a lower caste or as an animal, since the wheel of karma applies to both man and animals. Accordingly, all creatures, both man and beast, are in their current situations because of the actions (karma) of previous lives.

The Caste System

The caste system is a unique feature of the Hindu religion. The account of its origin is an interesting story. Brahma created Manu, the first man. From Manu came the four different types of people, as the creator Brahma determined. From Manu's head came the Brahmins, the best and most holy people. Out of Manu's hands came the Kshatriyas, the rulers and warriors. The craftsmen came from his thighs and are called Vaisyas. The remainder of the people came from Manu's feet and are known as Sudras. Therefore, the structure of the caste system is divinely inspired.

The Brahmins are honored by all the people, including the royal family. Their jobs as priests and philosophers are subsidized by the state and involve the study of their sacred books.

The Kshatriyas are the upper middle class involved in the government and professional life, but they are lower in status than the Brahmins.

The Vaisyas are the merchants and farmers below the Brahmins and Kshatriyas but above the rest of the population in their status and religious privileges.

The Sudras are the lowest caste whose duty is to serve the upper castes as laborers and servants. They are excluded from many of the religious rituals and are not allowed to study the vedas.

The caste system became more complicated as time went on, with literally thousands of subcastes coming into existence. Today the caste system is still an integral part of the social order of India, even though it has been outlawed by the Indian government.

Swami Vivekananda gives the rationale for the caste system:

> Caste is a natural order. I can perform one duty in social life, and you another; you can govern a country, and I can mend a pair of old shoes, but there is no reason why you are greater than I, for can you mend my shoes? Can I govern the country? I am clever in mending shoes, you are clever in reading, vedas, but there is no reason why you should trample on my head...Caste is good. That is the only natural way of solving life. Men must form themselves into groups, and you cannot get rid of that. Wherever you go there will be caste. But that does not mean that there should be these privileges. They should be knocked on the head. If you teach vedanta to the fisherman, he will say, I am as good a man as you, I am a fisherman, you are a philosopher, but I have the same God in me as you have in you. And that is what we want, no privileges for any one, equal chances for all; let every one be taught that the Divine is within, and every one will work out his own salvation...(*The Complete Works of Swami Vivekananda Almora*, Hollywood, CA: Vendanta Press, 1924-32, III: 245 f., 460).

Salvation

Salvation, for the Hindu, can be achieved in one of three ways: the way of works, the way of knowledge, or the way of devotion.

1.   *The Way of Works.* The way of works, *karma marga*, is the path to salvation through religious duty. It consists of carrying out the prescribed ceremonies, duties and religious rites. The Hindu believes that by doing these things he can add favorable karma to his merit. Moreover, if he does them religiously, he believes it is possible to be reborn as a Brahmin on his way toward liberation from the wheel of karma.

   The performance of these practices is something non-intellectual and emotionally detached, since it is the mechanical carrying out of prescribed laws and rituals. A basic concept in Hinduism is that one's actions, done in sincerity, must not be done for gain but must be done unselfishly.

2.   *The Way of Knowledge.* Another way of achieving

salvation—in the Hindu sense—is the way of knowledge. The basic premise behind the way of knowledge is the cause of human suffering based upon ignorance. This mental error concerning our own nature is at the root of mankind's problems. The error in man's thinking is this: man sees himself as a separate and real entity. The truth of the matter, Hindus say, is this: the only reality is Brahman, there is no other. Therefore, man, rather than being a separate entity, is part of the whole, Brahman.

Selfhood is an illusion. As long as man continues seeing himself as a separate reality he will be chained to the wheel of birth, death and rebirth. He must be saved from this wrong belief by the proper understanding that he has no independent self. This knowledge is not merely intellectual but experiential, for the individual reaches a state of consciousness where the law of karma is of no effect. This experience comes after much self-discipline and meditation. The way of knowledge does not appeal to the masses but rather to an intellectual few who are willing to go through the prescribed steps.

3. *The Way of Devotion*. The way of devotion, *bhakti*, is chronologically the last of the three ways of salvation. It is that devotion to a deity which may be reflected in acts of worship, both public and private. This devotion, based upon love for the deity, will also be carried out in human relationships; i.e., love of family, love of master, etc. This devotion can lead one to ultimate salvation. The *Bhagavad Gita* is the work which has devoted special attention to this way of salvation. This path to salvation is characterized by commitment and action.*

The Sacred Cow

From early times the Hindus revered the cow and considered it a possessor of great power. The following verses from the *atharva veda* praise the cow, identifying it with the entire visible universe:

Worship to thee, springing to life, and worship to thee when born!
Worship, O Cow, to thy tail-hair, and to thy hooves, and to thy form!

---

*We have combined *bhakti yoga* (devotion) and *raja yoga* (meditation). Some treat the two aspects as separate ways of salvation.

Hitherward we invite with prayer the Cow who pours a thousand streams,

By whom the heaven, by whom the earth, by whom these waters are preserved....

Forth from thy mouth the songs came, from thy neck's nape sprang strength, O Cow.

Sacrifice from thy flanks was born, and rays of sunlight from thy teats.

From thy fore-quarters and thy thighs motion was generated, Cow!

Food from thine entrails was produced, and from thy belly came the plants....

They call the Cow immortal life, pay homage to the Cow as Death.

She hath become this universe, Fathers, and Rishis, hath become the Gods, and men, and Spirits.

The man who hath this knowledge may receive the Cow with welcoming.

So for the giver willingly doth perfect sacrifice pour milk....

The Cow is Heaven, the Cow is Earth, the Cow is Vishnu, Lord of Life.

The heavenly beings have drunk the out-pourings of the Cow,

When these heavenly beings have drunk the out-pourings of the Cow,

They in the Bright One's dwelling-place pay adoration to her milk.

For Soma some have milked her; some worship the fatness she hath poured.

They who have given a Cow to him who hath this knowledge have gone up to the third region of the sky.

He who hath given a Cow unto the Brahmans winneth all the worlds.

For Right is firmly set in her, devotion, and religious zeal.

Both Gods and mortal men depend for life and being on the Cow.

She hath become this universe: all that the Sun surveys is she (*Atharva Veda* X:10).

Hinduism and Christianity

A comparison between Hinduism and Christianity shows the wide divergence of belief between the two faiths.

On the subject of God, Hinduism's supreme being is the undefinable, impersonal Brahman, a philosophical absolute. Christianity, on the other hand, teaches that there is a Supreme Being Who is the infinite-personal Creator. The God of Christianity, moreover, is loving and keenly interested in the affairs of mankind, quite in contrast to the aloof deity of Hinduism.

The Bible makes it clear that God cares about what happens to each one of us. "And call upon Me in the day of trouble; I shall rescue you, and you will honor Me" (Psalm 50:15 NASB). "Come to Me, all who are weary and heavy laden, and I will give you rest" (Matthew 11:28 NASB).

The Hindu views man as a manifestation of the impersonal Brahman, without individual self or self-worth. Christianity teaches that man was made in the image of God with a personality and the ability to receive and give love. Although the image of God in man has been tarnished by the fall, man is still of infinite value to God. This was demonstrated by the fact that God sent His only-begotten Son, Jesus Christ, to die to redeem sinful man, even while man was still in rebellion against God.

The Bible says, "For while we were still helpless, at the right time Christ died for the ungodly. For one will hardly die for a righteous man; though perhaps for the good man someone would dare even to die. But God demonstrates His own love toward us, in that while we were yet sinners, Christ died for us" (Romans 5:6-8 NASB). "Namely, that God was in Christ reconciling the world to Himself, not counting their trespasses against them, and He has committed to us the word of reconciliation. Therefore, we are ambassadors for Christ, as though God were entreating through us; we beg you on behalf of Christ, be reconciled to God. He made Him who knew no sin to be sin on our behalf, that we might become the righteousness of God in Him" (2 Corinthians 5:19-21 NASB).

In Hinduism there is no sin against a Holy God. Acts of wrongdoing are not done against any God but are mainly a result of ignorance. These evils can be overcome by following the guidelines of one's caste and way of salvation. To the contrary, Christianity sees sin as a real act of rebellion against a perfect and Holy God. All acts of transgression are ultimately acts of rebellion against the laws of God.

The Scripture states, "Against Thee, Thee only, I have

sinned, and done what is evil in Thy sight, so that Thou art justified when Thou dost speak, and blameless when Thou dost judge" (Psalm 51:4 NASB). "For all have sinned and fall short of the glory of God" (Romans 3:23 NASB).

Salvation in Hinduism can be attained in one of three general ways: the way of knowledge, knowing one is actually a part of the ultimate Brahman and not a separate entity; the way of devotion, which is love and obedience to a particular deity; or the way of works, or following ceremonial ritual. This salvation is from the seemingly endless cycle of birth, death, and rebirth. By contrast, in Christianity salvation is from a potentially eternal separation from God and cannot be obtained by any number of good deeds, but rather is given freely by God to all who will receive it.

The Bible says, "For by grace you have been saved through faith; and that not of yourselves, it is the gift of God; not as a result of works, that no one should boast" (Ephesians 2:8,9 NASB). "He saved us, not on the basis of deeds which we have done in righteousness, but according to His mercy, by the washing of regeneration and renewing by the Holy Spirit" (Titus 3:5 NASB). "He who believes in the Son has eternal life; but he who does not obey the Son shall not see life, but the wrath of God abides on him" (John 3:36 NASB).

Hinduism views the material world as transitory and of secondary importance to the realization of Brahman, while Christianity sees the world as having objective reality and its source in the creative will of God. Hindus see the world as an extension of Brahman, part of the absolute, while Christianity views the world as an entity eternally different in nature from God: not part of some universal or monistic One.

The Bible says that in the beginning God created the heavens and the earth (Genesis 1:1). Since the earth, therefore, was created by God, it is not to be identified with Him or His eternal nature.

These contradictions represent major diversities between the two religions. Many other differences remain which we cannot discuss in this small space. However, even with this limited spectrum of differences, one readily can see that the two faiths of Hinduism and Christianity never can be reconciled. The basic foundations on which both are built are mutually exclusive.

Hindu Terms

AGNI — The Vedic god of the altar fire who mediates between the gods and men. Mentioned in the Rig Veda.

ATMAN — The real self, the eternal and sometimes universal life principle.

BHAGAVAD-GITA — The "Song of the Lord," the most well-known of all Hindu scriptures. Contains a philosophical dialogue between the warrior Arjuna and the Lord God Krishna.

BRAHMA — The creator god, the first member of the Hindu triad, consisting of Brahma, Shiva, and Vishna.

BRAHMAN — Ultimate Reality, the supreme essence of the universe, the all-prevading deity.

BRAHMIN — (or Brahman) A member of the priestly caste, the highest and most noble class.

DHARMA — The teachings of virtue and principle. A term by which Hindus refer to their own religion.

GANESA — The god of prudence and wisdom represented as being a short red or yellow man with an elephant's head.

HANUMAN — The monkey god, lord of the winds. He helped Rama in battle.

INDRA — The Vedic god of rain and thunder, originally the god of light and once considered (during the Vaidic period) as a member of the Hindu triad. Not as important today as in the past.

KARMA — The culminating value of all of one's life actions, good and bad, which together determine one's next rebirth after death.

KRISHNA — The eighth or ninth incarnation of Vishnu, one of the most widely worshipped deities. Krishnaites believe Krishna is the supreme deity, incarnating as Vishnu.

LAKSHMI — Goddess of beauty and wealth, concubine of Krishna (and/or Vishnu).

MAHABHARATA—One of the national epics of India. Contained in the Mahabharata is the famous Bhagavad Gita.

MAYA—The power that produces the transient phenomena of physical existence.

MOKSHA—The term for liberation from the bondage of finite existence.

PARVATI—The goddess who is believed to be the daughter of the Himalayas. A consort of Shiva.

PURANAS—Part of the Hindu scriptures consisting of myths and legends mixed with historical events.

RAMAYANA—One of the national epics of India based upon the story of the good king Rama, who was purported to be an incarnation of the god Vishnu.

RISHI—First, an inspired poet or holy sage; later, any wise man.

SAMSARA—The cyclical transmigration or rebirth of souls passing on from one existence to another until release can be achieved.

SARASVATI—The goddess of learning, music and speech; the consort of Brahma.

SOMA—The soma plant is a leafless vine from Western India that yields an intoxicating juice. The personification of soma was once worshipped as a god.

UPANISHADS—Part of the Hindu sacred scriptures containing speculative treatises on the nature of ultimate reality and the way to achieve union with the absolute.

VARUNA—Hindu god, considered as ruler and guardian of the cosmic order.

VEDA—The oldest of the Hindu scriptures, consisting of four collections of sacred writings.

VISHNU—The preserver, second god of the Hindu triad.

YOGA—The Hindu path of union with the divine. Any sort of exercise (physical, mental, or spiritual) which promotes one's journey to union with Brahma.

YOGI—A devotee of yoga.

Hinduism Bibliography

Almore, Swami Vivekananda, *The Complete Works of*

Swami Vivekananda Almore, Hollywood, CA: Vedanta Press, 1924-1932, III.

Bowker, John, *Problems of Suffering in Religions of the World*, London: Cambridge University Press, 1970.

Gaer, Joseph, *What the Great Religions Believe*, New York: Dodd, Mead, and Company, 1963.

Nichols, Bruce in *The World's Religions*, Sir Norman Anderson, ed., Grand Rapids, MI: William B. Eerdmans Publishing Company, 1976.

Noss, John B., *Man's Religions*, New York: MacMillan Company, 1969.

Radhakrishnan, S., *East and West, the End of Their Separation*, New York: Allen & Unwin, Humanities Press, 1954.

Rice, Edward, *Eastern Definitions*, Garden City, NJ: Doubleday, 1980.

Sen, K. M., *Hinduism*, London: Gannon Publ., 1963.

Smith, Huston, *The Religions of Man*, New York: Harper and Row, 1958.

Jainism

Hinduism gave birth to three religious factions: Jainism, Buddhism and Sikhism. Jainism was its first offspring and though, like any child, it appears in a certain light to be somewhat like its mother, it eventually established itself as a new religion. Within the Hindu religion, Jainism started as a reformation movement but soon found itself as an independent religion based upon the teachings of its founder, Mahavira. Although relatively small in its number of adherents (3 million Indian followers) compared to other religions, Jainism has had an influence disproportionate to its size.

Founder Mahavira

Jainism, in contrast to Hinduism, is based upon a founder and leader known as Mahavira. This name actually is an honorific title signifying "great man." Tradition places the birth of Mahavira at 599 B.C. in northeastern India, which would make him a contemporary of Buddha. Tradition also relates that Mahavira was the second son of a rajah living in luxurious surroundings. He married and had one daughter.

When his parents died, Mahavira decided at the age of 30 to live a life of self-denial, pledging to deny himself the care of his body and not to speak for 12 years. After a short time, Mahavira put off the robe he wore and wandered naked through India receiving injuries from both man and beast. He wandered for 12 years until he reached enlightenment at the age of 42.

The *Sacred Books of the East* record, "During the thirteenth year, in a squatting position...exposing himself to the heat of the sun...with knees high and the head low, in deep meditation, in the midst of abstract meditation he reached nirvana, the complete and full, the unobstructed, infinite absolute" (F. M. Mueller, ed., *Sacred Books of the East*, Vol. 22, Oxford: Krishna Press, 1879-1910, p. 201).

After reaching enlightenment, Mahavira stopped living by himself and took on disciples, preaching his new-found belief. So he continued to live until the end of his life, at which time he was said to have over 14,000 monks in his brotherhood (Maurice Rawlings, *Life-Wish: Reincarnation: Reality or Hoax*, Nashville: Thomas Nelson Inc., 1981, p. 63).

Jainism's Debt to Hinduism

It must be stressed that Jainism did not appear in a religious vacuum. Jainism began as an heretical movement within Hinduism, but now can only be viewed as a distinct religion with reference to Hinduism. Mahavira held firmly to such Hindu beliefs as the law of moral retribution or karma and the transmigration of souls after death. There were, however, many points of disagreement between the two religions at the inception of Jainism. Herbert Stroup lists some of the differences between Hinduism and Jainism:

1. The doctrine of karma, the law of causation as applied to the moral sphere, seemed to him too rigid and restrictive, for within Hinduism its rule is absolute. He sought to lessen this rigidity and to find a practical measure of release from it.

2. The Hindu conception of rebirth came to mean, especially in the Upanishadic period, that individual souls do not possess real individuality. According to Hindu doctrine souls do not remain individualized in eternity, but become absorbed in Brahma. Mahavira strongly asserted the independence or autonomy of the individual soul.

3. Hinduism taught caste. In Mahavira's time these lines of social organization were still in the making, and he benefited to a considerable extent personally from the system. But he was strongly democratic, believing in the worth of all individuals. He taught the importance of a casteless society.

4. The priestly caste, as a result of the solidifying caste system, was clearly becoming the most influential group in Indian life. Mahavira was a member of the second or warrior caste. This had much to lose as the priesthood became dominant in the society, and a good deal of the impact of early Jainism was in opposition to the prominence of the priestly caste.

5. Particularly in the Vedic and Brahmanic periods, Hinduism was polytheistic. One hymn in the Vedic literature suggests that the gods may number as many as 3,333. Mahavira, in the simplicity of his character, was repelled by the extremes of Vedic polytheism. In fact, he did not teach the existence of a god at all.

6. Hinduism in the Vedic and Brahmanic period also taught the importance of animal sacrifices. These ceremonial occasions became complex affairs with large numbers of animals slaughtered. Mahavira may well have developed his emphasis upon harmlessness (*ahimsa*) to all living things in response to the excesses of animal sacrifice in his time (Herbert Stroup, *Four Religions of Asia*, New York: Harper and Row, 1968, p. 99).

Jainism and Belief in God

Mahavira was vehemently opposed to the idea of acknowledging or worshipping a supreme being. He once said:

> A monk or a nun should not say, "The god of the sky!" "The god of the thunderstorm!" "The god who begins to rain!" "May rain fall!" "May the crops grow!" "May the king conquer!" They should not use such speech. But, knowing the nature of things, he should say, "The air." "A cloud is gathered, or come down." "The cloud has rained." This is the whole duty (F. M. Mueller, ed., *op. cit.*, vol. 22, p. 152).

Later Jainism, however, did acknowledge and worship a deity: Mahavira himself became their object of worship.

Deification of Mahavira

Although Mahavira denied that any God or gods existed to be worshipped, he, like other religious leaders, was deified by his later followers. He was given the designation as the 24th Tirthankara, the last and greatest of the savior beings. Mahavira was regarded as having descended from heaven without sin and with all knowledge.

> He descended from heaven...The venerable ascetic Mahavira descended from the Great Vimana (palace of the gods) (*Ibid.*, pp. 189, 190).

> Having wisdom, Mahavira committed no sin himself...He meditated, free from sin and desire (*Ibid.*, p. 86, 87).

> He possessed supreme, unlimited, unimpeded knowledge and intuition (*Ibid.*, p. 257).

Self-Denial

Jainism is a religion of asceticism involving rigid self-denial. Salvation or liberation could be achieved only by ascetic practices. These practices for the monks are listed in the "Five Great Vows" and include the renunciation of: (1) killing living things, (2) lying, (3) greed, (4) sexual pleasure, and (5) worldly attachments.

The monks, according to Mahavira, were to avoid women entirely because he believed they were the cause of all types of evil:

> Women are the greatest temptation in the world. This has been declared by the sage. He should not speak of women, nor look at them, nor converse with them, nor claim them as his own, nor do their work (*Ibid.*, p. 48).

These five great vows could be fulfilled completely only by those Jains who were living the monastic life. Consequently, the laymen who practiced Jainism were given a more modified code to follow.

Non-violence

Central to Jainism is the practice of non-violence or *ahimsa*. The dedicated Jain is constrained to reverence life and is forbidden to take life even at the lowest level. The obvious consequence of this belief is strict vegetarianism. Farming is frowned upon since the process would inevitably involve killing of lower forms of life. Ahimsa has been summed up in the following statement:

> This is the quintessence of wisdom: not to kill anything (*Ibid.*, Vol. 45, p. 247).

The Principles of Jainism

Among the sacred books of Jainism, the 12 *angas* hold the foremost position. In the second anga, called *sutra-keit-anga*, the following sayings are contained which give insight into the nature of Jainism:

> Know what causes the bondage of the soul; and knowing, try to remove it.
>
> All things are eternal by their very nature.
>
> As imprisoned birds do not get out of their cage, so those ignorant of right or wrong do not get out of their misery.
>
> There are three ways of committing sins: by our actions; by authorizing others, and by approval.
>
> A sage leads a life as far removed from love as from hate.
>
> All living beings hate pain: therefore do not injure them or kill them. This is the essence of wisdom: not to kill anything.
>
> Leave off pride, anger, deceit and greed.
>
> Men suffer individually for the deeds they themselves have done.
>
> The wise man should consider that not he alone suffers; all creatures in the world suffer.
>
> Conceit is a very thin thorn; it is difficult to pull out.
>
> No man should seek fame and respect by his austerities.
>
> A man should treat all creatures in the world as he himself would like to be treated.
>
> He who is purified by meditation is like a ship in the water that avoids all dangers until it reaches the shore.
>
> Do not maintain that there is no such thing as good or evil, but that there is good and evil.

The reason most Jains are wealthy is that their devotion to ahimsa precludes their assuming most manual jobs. They were left to run such non-life-threatening occupations as finance, commerce, and banking.

Jainism and Christianity

Jainism is a religion of legalism, for one attains his own

salvation only through the path of rigid self-denial. There is no freedom in this religion, only rules. In contrast to this system which teaches salvation in the Hindu sense of the word (through self-effort), the biblical salvation sets one free through Jesus Christ, who said:

> If therefore the Son shall make you free, you shall be free indeed (John 8:36, NASB).
>
> Come to Me, all who are weary and heavy-laden, and I will give you rest. Take My yoke upon you, and learn from Me, for I am gentle and humble in heart; and you shall find rest for your souls. For My yoke is easy, and My load is light (Matthew 11:28-30, NASB).

The faith Jesus taught alleviates the burdens of people, while Jainism only adds to them.

Any concept of God in a personal sense is missing from Jainism. Mahavira and early Jainism rejected the idea of the existence of a supreme being. Although prayer and worship were not advocated by Mahavira himself, after his decease Jainism took to worshipping Mahavira and the Hindu deities.

The Bible condemns the worship of any other god apart from Yahweh. "I am the Lord your God, who brought you out of the land of Egypt, out of the house of slavery. You shall have no other gods before Me" (Exodus 20:2,3, NASB).

The doctrine of ahimsa, which is central to the Jain belief, is impossible to practice fully since there is no way to avoid killing millions of micro-organisms every time even a glass of water is drunk. This in turn should produce bad karma and thereby make any salvation virtually impossible.

Furthermore, there is no established source of authority for Jain beliefs in light of existing disputes over which of the various books are to be considered authoritative. These books did not even take any permanent form until 1,000 years after the death of Mahavira.

Contrast that with the evidence for the authority of the biblical documents, especially the New Testament. Sir Frederic Kenyon, former director and principal librarian of the British Museum, wrote this about the New Testament:

"The interval between the dates of original composition (of the New Testament) and the earliest extant evidence becomes so small as to be in fact negligible, and the last foundation for any doubt that the Scriptures have come down to us substantially as they were written has now been removed. Both the authenticity and the general integrity of the books of the New Testament may be regarded as finally established" (Sir Frederic Kenyon, *The Bible and Archaeology*, New York: Harper and Row, 1940, pp. 288, 289).

The failure of Jainism to advance much beyond certain areas of India speaks to the fact that it does not meet universal human need. This can be contrasted to Jesus Christ, whose impact is universal.

Turn to Me, and be saved, all the ends of the earth; For I am God and there is no other (Isaiah 45:22, NASB).

Jesus sent his disciples out with these words:

Go into all the world and preach the gospel to all creation (Mark 16:15, NASB).

...you shall be my witnesses both in Jerusalem, and in all Judea and Samaria, and even to the remotest part of the earth (Acts 1:8, NASB).

Griffith Thomas sums up the universal appeal of Christianity: "Other religions have had their ethical ideal of duty, opportunity, and even of love, but nowhere have they approached those of Christ, either in reality or in attractiveness or in power. Christ's message is remarkable for its *universal adaptation*. Its appeal is universal; it is adapted to all men from the adult down to the child; it makes its appeal to all times and not merely to the age in which it was first given. And the reason is that it emphasizes a threefold ethical attitude toward God and man which makes a universal appeal as nothing else does or perhaps can do. Christ calls for repentance, trust and love" (Griffith Thomas, *Christianity Is Christ*, Chicago: Moody Press, 1965, p. 35).

Comparison of Hinduism, Buddhism and Jainism

Hinduism, the mother religion, and its offshoots, Buddhism and Jainism, have much in common. However, on certain issues they sharply disagree. Robert E. Hume lists both the areas of agreement and disagreement between the faiths:

Points of Agreement between All Three Religions

General pessimism concerning the worth of human life in the midst of the material and social world.

The specific worthlessness of the human body.

The specific worthlessness of human activity.

The specific worthlessness of the individual as such.

A common tendency to ascetic monastic orders.

A common tendency to sectarian subdivisions.

No program of organized social amelioration.

A common ideal of the greatest good as consisting in subservience, quiescence or passivity, certainly not universally beneficial.

A common ideal of salvation to be obtained by methods largely negative or repressive, certainly not self-expressive.

A common appreciation of a certain religious value in sufferings borne, even voluntarily self-imposed, for self-benefit.

A common belief in many prophets in the same religion, teaching the same eternal doctrines of that particular system.

A common belief in karma and transmigration.

Points of Disagreement among the Three Religions

	NATURE OF EVIL	METHOD OF OVERCOMING EVIL	RESULTING SALVATION
Philosophic Hinduism:	Intellectual—ignorance of Brahma	By knowledge of pantheism	Mystical reabsorption into the Infinite
Jainism:	Physical—encumbrance of body	By asceticism of body	Freedom of soul from worldly attachments
Fundamental Buddhism:	Emotional—unsatisfied desires	By suppression of desires	Passionless peace, nirvana

	MATERIAL WORLD	INDIVIDUAL SOUL	SUPREME SOUL
Philosophic Hinduism:	Unreal, an illusion	Unreal, a temporary emanation	The only Real, the All
Jainism:	Real	Real	Unreal
Fundamental Buddhism:	Unreal	Unreal	Unreal

	VALUE OF ASCETICISM	VALUE OF MORALITY
Philosophic Hinduism:	Optional, though theoretically unnecessary	Unimportant; ultimately illusory
Jainism:	Obligatory; the chief means of salvation	Relatively unimportant; list of prohibitions
Fundamental Buddhism:	Of desires, rather than of only the body	Quite important; yet distinctly subordinate

(Robert E. Hume, *The World's Living Religions*, New York: Charles Scribner's Sons, rev. ed., 1959, pp. 82-84).

Jainistic Terms

AHIMSA — The practice of non-violence and reverence for life. Ahimsa forbids the taking of animal life at any level.

DIGAMBARAS — The sect of Jainism that insists on going naked, as did the Mahavira, when duty called for it.

FIVE GREAT VOWS — The principle of self-denial, central to Jain belief, which includes the renunciation of (1) killing living things, (2) lying, (3) greed, (4) sexual pleasure, (5) worldly attachments.

JAINS — The designation for the disciples of Mahavira the Jina (the Conqueror).

JINA — Literally, "the conqueror." The designation given to Mahavira for his achievement of victory over his bodily desires. His disciples were thus named Jains.

MAHAVIRA — An honorific title meaning "great man," given to the founder of Jainism.

NIRGRANTHA — Literally, "naked one." A person who practices asceticism in accordance with Jain principles.

SALLAKHANA — The rite of voluntary self-starvation which, according to tradition, took the life of Mahavira's parents.

SHVETAMBARAS — "The white clad," one of the two main sects of Jainism. The Shvetambaras are the liberal wing who believe in wearing at least one garment in contrast to the Digambaras, who insist on wearing nothing when duty demands.

STHANAKVASIS — A Jain sect that worships everywhere, not allowing for idols or temples.

TIRTHANKARA — A savior being. According to Jain belief, Mahavira is the 24th Tirthankara, the last and greatest of the savior beings.

TWELVE ANGAS — The part of the sacred scriptures of Jainism which holds the foremost position.

VENERABLE ONE — One of the titles given to the Mahavira by his later disciples.

Jainism Bibliography

Hume, Robert E., *The World's Living Religions*, New York: Charles Scribner's Sons, rev. ed., 1959.

Mueller, F. M., ed., *Sacred Books of the East*, vol. 22, Oxford: Krishna Press, 1879-1910.

Rawlings, Maurice, *Life-Wish: Reincarnation: Reality or Hoax*, Nashville: Thomas Nelson Inc., 1981.

Stroup, Herbert, *Four Religions of Asia*, New York: Harper and Row, 1968.

Buddhism

Buddhism began in India about 500 years before the birth of Christ. The people living at that time had become disillusioned with certain beliefs of Hinduism including the caste system, which had grown extremely complex. The number of outcasts (those who did not belong to any particular caste) was continuing to grow.

Moreover, the Hindu belief of an endless cycle of births, deaths and rebirths was viewed with dread. Consequently, the people turned to a variety of beliefs, including the worship of animals, to satisfy this spiritual vacuum. Many different sects of Hinduism arose, the most successful being that of Buddhism, which denies the authority of the vedas.

The Buddha

Buddhism, unlike Hinduism, can point to a specific founder. However, in Buddhism, like so many other religions, fanciful stories arose concerning events in the life of the founder, Siddhartha Gautama (fifth century B.C.):

> Works devoted to the exposition of philosophical doctrines or religions usually begin with the biography of the founder. Most of these biographies are, however, largely if not wholly mythical. The piety of the average disciples has never failed to make the sages whom they celebrate perform such impossible deeds as are calculated to increase their renown in

the eyes of the people, so that often enough within a few years of their death many of these masters are already seen to be transformed into mythological figures.

The Buddha was no exception. Archaeological discoveries have proved, beyond a doubt, his historical character, but apart from the legends we know very little about the circumstances of his life (Alexandra David-Neel, *Buddhism: Its Doctrines and Its Methods*, New York: St. Martin's Press, 1977, p. 15).

Though Buddha, as well as other religious leaders, was deified by later disciples, this was not the case with Jesus of Nazareth. The accounts of His miracles and His claims as to being God in human flesh were recorded from eyewitness testimony rather than having been developed over a long period of time. (See 1 John 1:1-3 and 2 Peter 1:16.)

Early Biography

The Buddha, or "enlightened one," was born about 560 B.C. in northeastern India. His family name was Gautama, his given name Siddhartha. Siddhartha was the son of a rajah, or ruler. His mother died when he was just a week old and Siddhartha was cared for by his mother's sister, who was also the rajah's second wife. There was supposedly a prophecy given at the time of his birth by a sage at his father's court.

The prophecy said that the child would be a great king if he stayed at home, but if he decided to leave home, he would become a savior for mankind. This bothered his father, for he wanted his son to succeed him as king. Therefore, to keep him at home, his father surrounded him with wealth and pleasures and kept all painful and ugly things out of his sight.

Siddhartha eventually married and had a son but was still confined to the palace and its pleasures. One day he informed his father that he wished to see the world. This excursion would forever change his life, for it was during this journey that he saw "the four passing sights."

Although his father ordered the streets to be cleansed and decorated and all elderly or infirmed people to stay inside, there were those who did not get the message. The first troubling sight Siddhartha saw was that of a decrepit old man. When Siddhartha asked what happened to this man, he was told that the man was old, as everyone someday would become.

Later, he met a sick man and was told that all people were liable to be sick and suffer pain like that individual.

He then saw a funeral procession with a corpse on its way to cremation, the followers weeping bitterly. When asked what that meant, the prince was informed that it was the way of life, for sooner or later both prince and pauper would have to die.

The last sight was that of a monk begging for his food. The tranquil look on the beggar's face convinced Siddhartha that this type of life was for him. Immediately he left the palace and his family in search of enlightenment. The night that he left his home to seek enlightenment became known as the Great Renunciation.

The former prince, now a beggar, spent his time wandering from place to place seeking wisdom. Unsatisfied by the truths taught in the Hindu scriptures, he became discouraged but continued on his quest. He tried asceticism but this gave him no peace. The fateful day in his life came while he was meditating beneath a fig tree.

Buddha's Enlightenment

Deep in meditation, he reached the highest degree of God-consciousness, known as nirvana. He supposedly stayed under the fig tree for seven days, after that, the fig tree was called the bodhi, or the bo tree, the tree of wisdom. The truths he learned he would now impart to the world, no longer as Siddhartha Gautama, but as the Buddha, the enlightened one.

When the Buddha emerged from his experience under the bo tree, he met with five monks who had been his companions. It was to these monks that the Buddha began his teaching ministry with the sermon at Benares. The sermon contained the following:

> These two extremes, monks, are not to be practiced by one who has gone forth from the world. What are the two? That conjoined with the passions and luxury, which is low, vulgar, common, ignoble, and useless; and that conjoined with self-torture, which is painful, ignoble, and useless. Avoiding these two extremes the Blessed One has gained the

enlightenment of the Middle Path, which produces insight and knowledge, and leads to calm, to higher knowledge, enlightenment, nirvana.

And what, monks, is the Middle Path...? It is the noble Eightfold Path: namely, right view, right intention, right speech, right action, right livelihood, right effort, right mindfulness, right concentration...

Now this, monks, is the noble truth of pain (dukkha): birth is painful, old age is painful, sickness is painful, death is painful, sorrow, lamentation, dejection, and despair are painful. Contact with unpleasant things is painful, not getting what one wishes is painful. In short the five components of existence are painful.

Now this, monks, is the noble truth of the cause of pain: the craving, which tends to rebirth, combined with pleasure and lust, finding pleasure here and there; namely, the craving for passion, the craving for existence, the craving for non-existence.

Now this, monks, is the noble truth of the cessation of pain, the cessation without a remainder of craving, the abandonment, forsaking, release, non-attachment.

Now this, monks, is the noble truth of the path that leads to the cessation of pain: this is the noble Eightfold Path (E. A. Burtt, ed., *The Teachings of the Compassionate Buddha*, New York: New American Library, 1955, pp. 29, 30).

After the sermon at Benares, the Buddha started to spread his teachings to the people of India. The Indian people, disillusioned with Hinduism, listened intently to this new doctrine. By the time of Buddha's death, at age 80, his teachings had become a strong force in India.

The Death of Buddha

The following discourse is from the Tripitaka. The dying Buddha is instructing a young monk against craving, one of the major doctrines of Theravada Buddhism:

I am old now, Ananda, and full of years: my journey nears its end, and I have reached my sum of days, for I am nearly eighty years old. Just as a worn out cart can only be kept going if it is tied up with thongs, so the body of the Tathagata can only be kept going by bandaging it.

Only when the Tathagata no longer attends to any outward object, when all separate sensations stops and he is deep in inner concentration, is his body at ease.

So, Ananda, you must be your own lamps, be your own refuges. Take refuge in nothing outside yourselves. Hold firm to the truth as a lamp and a refuge, and do not look for refuge to anything besides yourselves. A monk becomes his own lamp and refuge by continually looking on his body, feelings, perceptions, moods, and ideas in such a manner that he conquers the cravings and depressions of ordinary men and is always strenuous, self-possessed, and collected in mind. Whoever among my monks does this, either now or when I am dead, if he is anxious to learn, will reach the summit.

The Four Noble Truths and the Eightfold Path

The First Noble Truth is the existence of suffering. Birth is painful, and death is painful; disease and old age are painful. Not having what we desire is painful, and having what we do not desire is also painful.

The Second Noble Truth is the cause of suffering. It is the craving desire for the pleasures of the senses, which seeks satisfaction now here, now there; the craving for happiness and prosperity in this life and in future lives.

The Third Noble Truth is the ending of suffering. To be free of suffering one must give up, get rid of, extinguish this very craving, so that no passion and no desire remain.

The Fourth Noble Truth leads to the ending of all pain by way of the Eightfold Path.

The first step on that path is *Right Views:* You must accept the Four Noble Truths and the Eightfold Path.

The second step is *Right Resolve:* You must renounce the pleasures of the senses; you must harbor no ill will toward anyone and harm no living creature.

The third step is *Right Speech:* Do not lie; do not slander or abuse anyone. Do not indulge in idle talk.

The fourth is *Right Behavior:* Do not destroy any living creature; take only what is given to you; do not commit any unlawful sexual act.

The fifth is *Right Occupation:* You must earn your livelihood in a way that will harm no one.

The sixth is *Right Effort:* You must resolve and strive heroically to prevent any evil qualities from arising in you and to abandon any evil qualities that you may possess. Strive to acquire good qualities and encourage those you do possess to grow, increase and be perfected.

The seventh is *Right Contemplation:* Be observant,

strenuous, alert, contemplative, free of desire and of sorrow.

The eighth is *Right Meditation:* When you have abandoned all sensuous pleasures, all evil qualities, both joy and sorrow, you must then enter the four degrees of meditation, which are produced by concentration.

The Veneration of The Buddha

Some time after his death, the Buddha was deified by some of his followers. The following description of him is typical of the adulation he was given:

1. The countenance of the Buddha is like the clear full moon,
   Or again, like a thousand suns releasing their splendour.
   His eyes are pure, as large and as broad as a blue lotus.
   His teeth are white, even and close, as snowy as white jade.

2. The Buddha's virtues resemble the boundless great ocean.
   Infinite wonderful jewels are amassed within it.
   The calm, virtuous water of wisdom always fills it.
   Hundreds and thousands of supreme concentrations throng it.

3. The marks of the wheel beneath his feet are all elegant —
   The hub, the rim, and the thousand spokes which are all even.
   The webs on his hands and his feet are splendid in all parts —
   He is fully endowed with markings like the king of geese.

4. The Buddha-body's radiance is like a golden mountain's;
   It is clear, pure, peculiar, without equal or likeness,
   And it too has the virtues of beauty and loftiness.
   Therefore I bow my head to the Buddha, king of mountains.

5. His marks and signs are as unfathomable as the sky.
   And they surpass a thousand suns releasing their splendour.

All like a flame or a phantom are inconceivable.
Thus I bow my head to him whose mind has no at-
tachments
(Richard Robinson, trans., *Chinese Buddhist Verse*,
London: Greenwood Publ., 1954, p. 48).

Such veneration of the Buddha is against the basic
teachings of Buddha himself.

Theravada and Mahayana Buddhism

Early Buddhism was confined largely to India and is
usually referred to as Theravada Buddhism. Later Buddhism, which became very popular outside of India
(notably in China and Japan), became known as Mahayana
Buddhism:

By the time of King Asoka (c. 236-232 B.C.), Indian Buddhism had split into a number of groups generally referred to
as Theravada schools. Again, around the beginning of the
Christian era, Mahayana Buddhism arose, being distinguished from Theravada Buddhism primarily by its enlarge-
ment of the bodhisattva ideal, according to which certain
compassionate beings or bodhisattvas defer their own emancipation in order to save others, and by its consequent en-
largement of the offer of salvation, making it available not
only to those who enter monastic orders but to all who trust
in a bodhisattva.

For several centuries Buddhism continued to evolve in
India, developing in interaction with the various Indian
religions and philosophies, but due to the Islamic invasion of
the thirteenth century, it ceased to exist in the land of its
birth (Agency for Cultural Affairs, *Japanese Religion: A
Survey*, Tokyo, New York and San Francisco: Kodansha
International Ltd., 1972, 1981, p. 48).

As we can see from the comparative chart, on the next
page, Mahayana Buddhism had many qualities which
differed from Theravada Buddhism but which were very
attractive to new converts:

Theravada	Mahayana
Man as an individual	Man as involved with others
Man on his own in the universe (emancipation by self-effort)	Man not alone (salvation by grace)
Key virtue: wisdom	Key virtue: *karuna*, compassion
Religion: a full-time job (primarily for monks)	Religion: relevant to life in the world (for laymen as well)
Ideal: the Arhat	Ideal: the Bodhisattva
Buddha: a saint	Buddha: a savior
Eschews metaphysics	Elaborates metaphysics
Eschews ritual	Includes ritual
Confines prayer to meditation	Includes petitionary prayer
Conservative	Liberal

(Huston Smith, *The Religions of Man*, New York: Harper and Row, 1958, p. 138).

Nirvana

A key concept in Buddhism is nirvana, the final goal for the Buddhists. Donald K. Swearer gives insight to this important concept.

> Nirvana has been a troublesome idea for students of Buddhism. Just what is it? The term itself does not offer much help. Like not-self (*an-atta*), nirvana is a negative term. Literally, it means the "blowing out" of the flame of desire, the negation of suffering (*dukkha*). This implies that nirvana is not to be thought of as a place but as a total reorientation or state of being realized as a consequence of the extinction of blinding and binding attachment. Thus, at least, nirvana implies that the kind of existence one has achieved is inconceivable in the ordinary terms of the world (Donald K. Swearer, *Buddhism*, Niles, IL: Argus Communications, 1977, p. 44).

The following texts mention nirvana:

> Dispassion is called the Way. It is said: "Through dispassion is one freed." Yet, in meaning, all these (words: stopping, renunciation, surrender, release, lack of clinging) are synonyms for nirvana. For, according to its ultimate meaning, nirvana is the Aryan Truth of the stopping of suffering (Edward Conze, et. al, *Buddhist Texts Through the*

Ages, New York: Philosophical Library, 1954, "Path of Purity 507," p. 100).

"Venerable Nagasena, things produced of karma are seen in the world, things produced of cause are seen, things produced of nature are seen. Tell me, what in the world is born not of karma, not of cause, not of nature" (*Ibid.*, "The Questions of King Milinda," p. 97).

There is, monks, that plane where there is neither extension nor...motion nor the plane of infinite space...nor that of neither-perception-nor-non-perception, neither this world nor another, neither the moon nor the sun. Here, monks, I say that there is no coming or going or remaining or deceasing or uprising, for this is itself without any support...

There is, monks, an unborn, not become, not made, uncompounded, and...because there is,...an escape can be shown for what is born, has become, is made, is compounded (*Ibid.*, "Udana 81," pp. 94, 95).

Swearer comments on these passages:

These three passages point to different aspects of the concept of nirvana. The first passage illustrates our initial claim about nirvana, namely, that it is the negation of attachment and suffering (dukkha). The second, a question from King Milinda, is answered, as you probably guessed, by nirvana. Nirvana, then, is the one thing that is not caused by anything else. The third quotation pushes this idea even further. Nirvana as the Absolute Truth cannot be adequately expressed in words. Nonetheless, the term implies that there is a goal to be reached and that this goal surpasses anything experienced in this world of conventional understanding (Swearer, *op. cit.*, p. 45).

Sacred Scriptures

In Theravada Buddhism there are three groups of writings considered to be holy scripture, known as "The Three Baskets" (Tripitaka). The Vinaya Pitaka (discipline basket) contains rules for the higher class of Buddhists; the Sutta Pitaka (teaching basket) contains the discourses of the Buddha; and the Abidhamma Pitaka (metaphysical basket) contains Buddhist theology. The total volume of these three groups of writings is about 11 times larger than the Bible.

In Mahayana Buddhism the scriptures are much more voluminous, as Clark B. Offner reveals:

"A Mahayanist is one who reads Mahayana scriptures" is the definition given by one ancient Buddhist scholar. In contrast to the comparatively limited scope of the Pali canon used by Theravada Buddhists, Mahayana scriptures have multiplied to the point where standard editions of the Chinese canon encompass over 5,000 volumes. While the oldest scriptures are based on Sanskrit and contain much that is parallel to the Pali canon, other scriptures which have no Sanskrit prototypes have been written in Nepalese, Tibetan and Chinese.

Since there are no clear limits to the Mahayana "canon," comparatively recent works by later innovators are often given *de facto* canonical status in the sects which adhere to their teachings. As there are such a number and such a variety of scriptures, most Mahayana sects have chosen certain favourite ones to which they refer exclusively. The fact is that some such selection is necessary, for this extreme bulk and breadth of the scriptures make it impossible for believers to be acquainted with, let alone understand and practise, the often contradictory teachings found in them (Clark B. Offner, in *The World's Religions*, Sir Norman Anderson, ed., Grand Rapids: William B. Eerdmans Publishing Company, 1976, p. 181).

The Laity

Conze explains how the laity can gain religious merit:

The layman's one and only religious task at present can be to increase his store of merit. The Buddhist religion offers him four avenues for doing so:

1. He must observe the five precepts, or at least some of them. On feast days, every fortnight, he may add to them another three, i.e., he fasts, avoids worldly amusements, and uses neither unguents nor ornaments. A few observed still two more precepts, i.e., they did not sleep on a high, big bed and they accepted no gold or silver.

2. He must have devotion for the Three Treasures and faith is the virtue apposite to a householder's state of life. But this faith is not an exclusive one and does not entail a rejection of his ancestral beliefs and of the Brahmanic religious usages of his social environment. The Triple Jewel is not a jealous God and is not displeased by the worship of the deities of a man's country or caste.

3. He must be generous, especially to the monks, and give as much as possible to them, not only for their upkeep,

but also for religious buildings inhabited by no one. To some extent the merit produced by gifts depends on the spiritual endowments of the recipient, and therefore the sons of Sākyamuni, and in particular the Arhats, are the best possible "field for planting merit."

4. He may worship the relics of the Buddha. The actual attitude of the Buddhists to these teeth and bones is difficult to describe in terms readily understood in the West. It is obviously impossible for them to "pray" to the Buddha, for the reason that He is no longer there, being in nirvana, i.e., extinct as far as this world is concerned (Edward Conze, *A Short History of Buddhism*, London: George Allen and Unwin Ltd., 1980, p. 39).

Buddhist Precepts

There are five precepts taught by Buddhism that all Buddhists should follow:

1. Kill no living thing (including insects).
2. Do not steal.
3. Do not commit adultery.
4. Tell no lies.
5. Do not drink intoxicants or take drugs.

There are other precepts that apply only to monks and nuns. These include:

6. Eat moderately and only at the appointed time.
7. Avoid that which excites the senses.
8. Do not wear adornments (including perfume).
9. Do not sleep in luxurious beds.
10. Accept no silver or gold.

A Buddhist Creed

In 1981, Colonel H. S. Olcott, one of the founding presidents of the Theosophical Society, proposed a common platform for all Buddhist schools of thought. Various representatives of different Buddhist persuasions reviewed his work and found it to be satisfactory. It was published as an appendix to his *Buddhist Catechism*. The fundamental Buddhistic beliefs are:

1. Buddhists are taught to show the same tolerance, forbearance, and brotherly love to all men, without distinction; and an unswerving kindness towards the members of the animal kingdom.

2. The Universe was evolved, not created; and it functions according to law, not according to the caprice of any God.

3. The truths upon which Buddhism is founded are natural. They have, we believe, been taught in successive kalpas, or world periods, by certain illuminated beings called Buddhas, the name Buddha meaning "enlightened."

4. The fourth teacher in the present kalpa was Sakya Muni, or Guatama Buddha, who was born in a royal family in India about 2,500 years ago. He is an historical personage and his name was Siddhartha Gautama.

5. Sakya Muni taught that ignorance produces desire, unsatisfied desire is the cause of rebirth, and rebirth the cause of sorrow. To get rid of sorrow, therefore, it is necessary to escape rebirth; to escape rebirth, it is necessary to extinguish desire; and to extinguish desire, it is necessary to destroy ignorance.

6. Ignorance fosters the belief that rebirth is a necessary thing. When ignorance is destroyed the worthlessness of every such rebirth, considered as an end in itself, is perceived, as well as the paramount need of adopting a course of life by which the necessity for such repeated births can be abolished. Ignorance also begets the illusive and illogical idea that there is only one existence for man, and the other illusion that this one life is followed by states of unchangeable pleasure or torment.

7. The dispersion of all this ignorance can be attained by the persevering practice of an all-embracing altruism in conduct, development of intelligence, wisdom in thought, and destruction of desire for the lower personal pleasures.

8. The desire to live being the cause of rebirth, when that is extinguished rebirths cease and the perfected individual attains by meditation that highest state of peace called nirvana.

9. Sakya Muni taught that ignorance can be dispelled and sorrow removed by the knowledge of the four Nobel Truths, viz:

    1. The miseries of existence;
    2. The cause productive of misery, which is the desire ever renewed of satisfying oneself without being able ever to secure that end;

3. The destruction of that desire, or the estranging of oneself from it;

4. The means of obtaining this destruction of desire. The means which he pointed out is called the Noble Eightfold Path, viz: Right Belief; Right Thought; Right Speech; Right Action; Right Means of Livelihood; Right Exertion; Right Remembrance; Right Meditation.

10. Right Meditation leads to spiritual enlightenment, or the development of that Buddha-like faculty which is latent in every man.

11. The essence of Buddhism as summed up by the Tathagata (Buddha) himself is:
>   To cease from all sin,
>   To get virtue,
>   To purify the heart

12. The universe is subject to a natural causation known as "karma." The merits and demerits of a being in past existences determine his condition in the present one. Each man, therefore, has prepared the causes of the effects which he now experiences.

13. The obstacles to the attainment of good karma may be removed by the observance of the following precepts, which are embraced in the moral code of Buddhism, viz: (1) Kill not; (2) Steal not; (3) Indulge in no forbidden sexual pleasure; (4) Lie not; (5) Take no intoxicating or stupefying drug or liquor. Five other precepts, which need not here be enumerated, should be observed by those who would attain more quickly than the average layman the release from misery and rebirth.

14. Buddhism discourages superstitious credulity. Gautama Buddha taught it to be the duty of a parent to have his child educated in science and literature. He also taught that no one should believe what is spoken by any sage, written in any book, or affirmed by a tradition, unless it accord with reason.

Drafted as a common platform upon which all Buddhists can agree (Cited by Christmas Humphreys, *Buddhism*, London: Penguin Books, 1951, pp. 71-73).

Sayings of the Buddha

The following extracts are from the Dhammadada, which contains a collection of sayings attributed to the Buddha:

VIGILANCE is the way of immortality (the Deathless). Heedlessness is the way of death. Those that are vigilant do not die. Those that are heedless are already as though dead.

Those who know these things, those who know how to meditate, they take this delight in meditation, and in the knowledge of the noble.

By meditation and perseverance, by tireless energy, the wise attain to nirvana, the supreme beatitude.

He who meditates earnestly, he who is pure in conduct and mindful of every action, he who is self-restrained and righteous in his life, the fame of such a one shall increase.

By diligent attention, by reflection, by temperance, by self-mastery, the man of understanding makes for himself an island that no flood can overwhelm.

Do not give yourselves over to heedlessness. Have naught to do with the lusts of the flesh. The vigilant man, who is given to meditation, he will attain to abundant happiness.

When the wise man in his vigilance puts away heedlessness and ascends the tower of wisdom, he looks down, being free from sorrow, upon the sorrow-laden race of mankind. As from a mountain-top, the wise man looks down upon the foolish men in the valley.

Vigilant among the heedless, waking among those who slumber, as a fleet courser outstrips a sorry nag, so the wise go their way.

By yourselves must the effort be made: the Tathâgatas do but make known the way.

Conquer wrath with benevolence, overcome evil with good. Confound the niggardly with liberality, and with truth the speaker of falsehoods.

Even as a solid rock is unshaken by the wind, so are the wise unmoved by praise or by blame.

Whoso seeks his own welfare by devising injury to another, he is entangled in hatred, and does not attain to freedom.

Let your words be truth, and give not way to anger; give of your little to him that asks of you; by these three things men go to the realm of the gods.

He who refrains from action when it is the time to act, he who in his youth and strength, gives himself over to idleness, he whose will and whose spirit are feeble, this slothful man shall never find the way that leads to Wisdom.

Stem the torrent with all thy might, O Brahmana. Having understood how the formations (*samskaras*) are dissolved, thou wilt understand that which is not formed (which is not a group of impermanent elements).

It is not plaited hair, nor birth, nor wealth that makes the Brahmana. He in whom truth and justice reside, he is happy, he is a Brahmana.

Of what avail thy plaited hair, O witless one? Of what avail thy goatskin garment? Within there is disorder: thou carest only for the outer man.

I do not call him "a Brahmana" who is born of such a family or such a mother. He may be arrogant, he may be rich. He who is poor and detached from all things — him I call a Brahmana.

He who has shattered all bonds, he who is inaccessible to fear, he who is free from all servitude and cannot be shaken — him I call a Brahmana.

He who has broken the thong, the cord, and the girth, he who has destroyed all obstacles, he who is the Awakened — him I call a Brahmana.

He from whom the delights of the senses fall away as water from the petal of the lotus or a mustard seed from the point of a needle — him do I call Brahmana.

He who in this world has been able to set a term to his suffering, he who has set down his burden, he whom nothing can trouble, him do I call a Brahmana.

He whose knowledge is profound, he who possesses wisdom, who discerns the right path from the wrong, who has attained the highest aim, him do I call a Brahmana.

He who holds himself apart, both from laymen and from monks, who contents himself with little and does not beat upon other men's doors — him do I call a Brahmana.

He who uses no violence, whether to the weak or the strong, who neither slays nor causes to be slain — him do I call a Brahmana.

He who is tolerant with the intolerant, gentle with the violent, without greed among the grasping — him do I call a Brahmana.

He from whom envy, hatred, pride and hypocrisy have fallen away like a mustard-seed placed on the point of a needle — him do I call a Brahmana.

He whose speech is instructive and truthful and without harshness, offending none — him do I call a Brahmana.

He who no longer covets aught, whether in this world or

another, he who is unattached and inaccessible to trouble —
him do I call a Brahmana.

He who is free from all ties, whom knowledge preserves
from questioning, who has attained to the depths where
death is not — him do I call a Brahmana.

He who in this world has shaken off the two chains; the
chain of Good and the chain of Evil; who is pure and exempt
from suffering and passion — him do I call a Brahmana.

He who in his serenity, his purity, his changeless peace is
radiant as the flawless moon, who has dried up within him
the source of all joy — him do I call a Brahmana.

He who has traversed the miry path, the inextricable
world, so difficult to traverse, and all its vanities, he also,
having achieved the passage, and has reached the further
shore, who is meditative, unshaken, exempt from doubts,
unattached and satisfied — him do I call a Brahmana.

He who, putting off all human ties, has risen above all
divine ties, who has liberated himself from every tie — him do
I call a Brahmana.

He who has rejected that which causes pleasure and that
which causes suffering, he who is impassive, liberated from
all germs, the hero who has raised himself above all the
worlds — him do I call a Brahmana.

Nichiren Shoshu Buddhism

One form of Buddhism that has seen a revival of sorts in
the past 50 years is a Japanese mystical sect known as
Nichiren Shoshu. Its recent growth has been astounding,
as chronicled by Walter Martin:

Nichiren Shoshu continued as a small sect of Buddhism until
the founding in Japan of the Soka Gakkai (Value Creation
Society), by Makiguchi Tsunesaburo in 1930. Known first as
Soka Kyoiku Gakkai and founded by Makiguchi Tsunesaburo
and Josei Toda, Sokka Gakkai is the Japanese lay organization
of Nichiren Shoshu and has become the evangelistic arm of
the religion.

When the Japanese government attempted to unify all of
Japan under Shinto Buddhism in 1940, only Nichiren Shoshu
refused to obey. (NSB claims to be the only orthodox sect
among the many sects claiming Nichiren Daishonin as their
founders.) In 1940 there were only 21 members, all of whom
were arrested. Nineteen of those members converted to
Shintoism and were released. Leader Makiguchi died in

prison, and the only remaining member, Josei Toda, was released from prison in 1945, shortly before the end of World War Two.

Under Toda's leadership, the movement began growing and elected Toda the second president of Soka Gakki. In 1960 Daisaku Ikeda was inaugurated president over 1.3 million members. Ikeda expanded NSB's evangelism in foreign countries, opening a branch in the United States in 1960. The quickly growing branch of the sect held its first convention in 1963 in Chicago, with representatives from ten chapters. By 1973, membership was more than 250,000. From 1960 to 1973, NSB in the United States increased three-hundredfold! Japanese growth was even faster. The number of practicing Japanese families grew from three thousand in 1951 to more than seven million in 1971 (Walter Martin, ed., *The New Cults*, Santa Ana, CA: Vision House Publishers Inc., 1980, p. 323).

The origins of Nichiren Shoshu go back to a Japanese reformer named Nichiren Daishonon, who lived in the 13th century A.D.

Nichiren

Nichiren was born the son of a fisherman in Japan in A.D. 1222 (and died in A.D. 1282) during a time of turmoil in Japan. Christmas Humphreys sets the historical background of the time of Nichiren's birth:

In the last half of the twelfth century, the Kyoto Government had so degenerated that civil war broke out. After fifty or more bloody years of strife, in which Buddhist monasteries were more than once engaged, a few of the stronger feudal lords gained power, and after fighting each other to a standstill left the Minamoto family, with the great Yorimoto at its head, in control at the new capital of Kamakura. Thereafter, until 1868, the Emperor was more or less a puppet, and Japan was ruled by hereditary Shoguns.

The civil wars had developed and perfected the cult of Bushido, the eastern equivalent of the western cult of knighthood, and the cult was ripe for spiritual guidance. The existing Buddhist sects, discredited to some extent by participation in the political wars of Kyoto, were not suited to the needs of the new capital, and the people as a whole, as well as their feudal overlords, needed new forms of Buddhism. The need produced the supply, and within a century three new schools arose, the *Jodo* of China, elaborated in

Japan into *Jodo-Shin* or *Shin*, the Chinese *Ch'an*, now to be known as *Zen*, and the School of the firebrand Nichiren (1222-1282) (Christmas Humphreys, *op. cit.*, pp. 174, 175).

Nichiren studied the various schools of Buddhism until deciding upon which of the teachings were true. He was convinced that the true faith was taught by Dengyo Daishi (named Saicho before his death) who had introduced Tendai Buddhism to Japan in the eighth century. Dengyo Daishi taught that only one scripture was of supreme authority, the Lotus Sutra. Nichiren believed if he could get his people back to the Lotus Sutra, which he believed was the true interpretation of the words of Buddha, the country could be saved.

Nichiren went about preaching his newly discovered truth, condemning all others as false religions. This did not go over well with the authorities, making Nichiren the object of persecution. Nichiren was both arrested and exiled for his preaching, many times narrowly escaping with his life. At the time of his death in 1282 he had attracted many followers to his rediscovered truth.

The Lotus Sutra

Nichiren believed that the Lotus Sutra contained the true teaching of the Buddha, but the facts contradict his belief. The Lotus Sutra was composed somewhere between the second century B.C. and the second century A.D. The work differs in several aspects from traditional Buddhist beliefs. Edward Rice elaborates:

> The work stresses the eternal Buddha-principle, represented in innumerable forms to work out the salvation of all suffering humanity. In the Lotus Sutra, Buddha is the eternal, omniscient, omnipotent, omnipresent; creator-destroyer, re-creator of all worlds — concepts borrowed from Hinduism and carried over into Mahayana Buddhism...* Its central thesis is that of universal salvation: Everyone and everything have within the potentiality of Buddhahood (Edward Rice, *Eastern Definitions*, New York: Doubleday, 1980, p. 238).

The following is an extract from the Lotus Sutra:

---

* See our earlier section on the two main branches of Buddhism.

Those among the living beings,
Who have come into contact with former Buddhas,
And have learned the Law and practiced charity,
Or have held on to discipline and endured forbearance and humiliation,
Or have made serious efforts at concentration and understanding,
Or have cultivated various kinds of blessing and wisdom —
All such beings as these
Have already achieved Buddhahood...
Men who possess a tender heart...
Those who have offered relics,
Or have built hundreds of millions of pagodas....
Those who have had pictures of the Buddha embroidered,
Expressing the great splendor
Which he achieved from a hundred merits and blessings,
Whether embroidered by himself or by others,
Have all achieved Buddhahood.
Even boys at play
Who have painted Buddha figures
With straws, wooden sticks, brushes, or finger nails —
All people such as these,
By gradual accumulation of merits
And with an adequate sense of compassion,
Have already achieved Buddhahood.

Worship

Central to Nichiren Shoshu belief is the "gohonzon." The gohonzon is a black wooden box containing the names of important people in the Lotus Sutra and is used as a private altar. The gohonzon supposedly contains universal forces that control the devotee's life. There is, they believe, a direct connection between events in a person's life and the treatment of the gohonzon.

The worship ritual practiced by Nichiren Shoshu members is called "gongyo." The practice consists of kneeling before the gohonzon, the recitation of passages from the Lotus Sutra, then the rubbing of rosary-type beads while chanting the daimoku — "nam-myoho-renge-kyo."

The chief object of worship in Nichiren Shoshu Buddhism is a shrine known as the Dai-gohonzon located at the base of Mount Fuji in Japan. The individual gohonzons are mystical representations of the Dai-gohonzon.

Missionary Emphasis

Nichiren Shoshu's recent accelerated growth (1970 figures by the Japanese Office of Cultural Affairs put membership at over 16 million*) can be attributed directly to its missionary emphasis. Their members practice a proselytizing method called "Shakubuku," their goal being to convert the world to the one true faith:

> Sōka Gakkai regards itself as not only the one true Buddhist religion, but the one true religion on earth. Its principal aims are the propagation of its gospel throughout the world, by forced conversion if necessary, and the denunciation and destruction of all other faiths as "false" religions...Sōka Gakkai is unmistakably a church militant in Japan geared for a determined march abroad. Its significance to America and all nations cannot be ignored. Its target is world domination (Richard Okamoto, "Japan," *Look*, September 10, 1963, p. 16).

Zen Buddhism

Zen is a branch of Mahayana Buddhism that has become widely known in the West.

> The Chinese added to the many schools of Buddhism a new school, whose name reveals its history. Dhyana is the Indian word for meditation; it was changed in China to Chan and in Japan to Zen, which is now the best-known title of this sect (Elizabeth Seeger, *Eastern Religions*, New York: Crowell, 1973, p. 145).

The exact origin of Zen is unknown. Legend has it that Zen's teaching was derived from Bodhidharma, a wandering Buddhist master living in India 600 years before Christ. Bodhidharma supposedly told a Chinese emperor that the basic tenets of Buddhism are not dependent upon the scriptures; its teachings were directly transmitted from mind to mind and do not need to be explained in words. This sums up Zen's unorthodox approach to its teaching, for they have no sacred literature which they use for their instruction but employ any writings, Buddhistic or not, they deem necessary to further their religion. Bodhidharma summed up the Zen viewpoint with this famous saying:

---

* Agency for Cultural Affairs, *op. cit.*, p. 208.

A special tradition outside the scriptures,
No dependence on words,
A direct pointing at man,
Seeing into one's own nature and the attainment of wisdom

Development

Zen actually developed about one thousand years after the death of the Buddha. However, it contains Buddha's emphasis on meditation which led to his enlightenment. One statement attributed to the Buddha has become a frequent reference by Zen teachers: "Look within, you are the Buddha."

This goes along with Buddha's deathbed statement that his disciples must find their own ways through self-effort. This self-effort is the foundation of Zen practice, for only through disciplined individual work can one attain enlightenment, known in Zen as "Kensho" or "Satori."

Zen has found great popularity in the West, with a large selection of literature available on the subject, including such titles as *Zen and the Art of Motorcycle Maintenance*, *The Zen of Seeing*, and *Zen and Creative Management*. The list of titles is long and varied.

One famous story tells about a man who desired to be a Zen master. He asked to be taught Zen. The Zen master did not speak but began to pour a cup of tea for his visitor, using a cup that was already filled. The extra tea overflowed and ran across the table to drip to the rice-mat-covered floor. Still the Zen master kept pouring until the pot was empty. He finally spoke: "You are like this cup," he said. "You are full. How can I pour Zen into you? Empty yourself and come back."

Zazen

Central to Zen practice is *zazen*. Zazen is the method of sitting in Zen meditation, which is done daily at specific times with occasional periods of intense meditation lasting one week. The goal is final enlightenment. The practice of zazen is done under the guiding hand of a master (roshi). Nancy Wilson-Ross elucidates:

> The very heart of Zen practice lies in zazen, or sitting meditation done at specific times daily, with longer and more intensive periods on occasions of sesshin, in which con-

centrated "sitting" may endure for as long as a week. Zazen is a formalized procedure which consists of active meditation interspersed with the chanting of sutras. In this daily Zen chanting the sutra known as the *Prajna Paramita* is always included. The actual sitting itself is preceded by prescribed use of bells, wooden clappers and the exchange of formal bows. Practitioners sit facing a wall or the center of the zendo, depending on the tradition of the specific sect to which the group belongs or the preference of the presiding Zen roshi.

The usual zazen posture is the full lotus or half-lotus cross-legged sitting position on a specific type of round cushion. The position of the hands is strictly specified: they are held in front of the abdomen, the back of the left in the palm of the right, the thumbs lightly touching. The eyes are not closed, although the gaze is directed downward and is fixed a little in advance of the sitter. Zazen is terminated by the sound of wooden clappers, the ringing of a bell three times and the chanting of the Four Great Vows. Periods of formal sitting may be interspersed by walking meditation, known as *kinhin*. This is essentially a method for giving the body relief from the prolonged sitting posture, but it serves also as a way of practicing concentration, whether during a slow circling of the zendo or in a brisk walk outside (Nancy Wilson-Ross, *Buddhism: A Way of Thought*, New York, Alfred A. Knopf, Inc., 1980, p. 143).

The Koan

The master, in attempting to aid his pupil toward enlightenment, gives him a verbal puzzle known as a *koan*. Solving the koan supposedly leads the pupil into greater self-awareness. Commonly used koans by Zen masters number about 1,700, each of which may have hundreds of "answers" depending upon the exact circumstances of the students' training, Knowing the answer is not nearly as important as experiencing or realizing the answer. The following are some examples of koans:

A master, Wu Tsu, says, "Let me take an illustration from a fable. A cow passes by a window. Its head, horns, and the four legs all pass by. Why did not the tail pass by?"

What was the appearance of your face before your ancestors were born?

We are all familiar with the sound of two hands clapping. What is the sound of one hand? (If you protest that one hand can't clap, you go back to the foot of the class. Such a remark simply shows you haven't even begun to get the point.)

Li-ku, a high government officer of the T'ang dynasty, asked a famous Ch'an master: "A long time ago a man kept a goose in a bottle. It grew larger and larger until it could not get out of the bottle anymore. He did not want to break the bottle, nor did he wish to hurt the goose; how would you get it out?"

The master called out, "O Officer!"

"Yes," was the response.

"There, it's out!"

A monk asked Chao-chou, "What is the meaning of Bodhidharma's visit to China?" "The cypress tree in the courtyard," replied Bodhidharma.

A monk asked Thich Cam Thanh, "What is Buddha?" "Everything." The monk then asked, "What is the mind of Buddha?" "Nothing has been hidden." The monk said again, "I don't understand." Cam Thanh replied, "You missed!"

Satori

In Zen the sudden illumination or enlightenment is known as *satori*. Satori is an experience beyond analyzation and communication, bringing the practitioner into a state of maturity. The experience of satori comes abruptly and momentarily, but it can be repeated. It cannot be willed into existence.

Evaluation

Huston Smith gives an insightful evaluation of Zen belief:

Entering the Zen outlook is like stepping through Alice's looking glass. One finds oneself in a topsy-turvy wonderland in which everything seems quite mad—charmingly mad for the most part but mad all the same. It is a world of bewildering dialogues, obscure conundrums, stunning paradoxes, flagrant contradictions, and abrupt non sequiturs, all carried off in the most urbane, cheerful and innocent style (Huston Smith, *op. cit.*, p. 140).

Part of Zen's attraction is that one is not required to be responsible in evaluating anything in the world or even in his own thoughts. One loses his capacity to think logically and critically. While the Bible commands

Christians to test *all* things (1 Thessalonians 5:21, 22), Zen mocks critical analysis.

Buddhism and Christianity

There are radical differences between Buddhism and Christianity that make any attempt of reconciliation between the two faiths impossible. The Buddhistic world view is basically monistic. That is, the existence of a personal creator and Lord is denied. The world operates by natural power and law, not divine command.

Buddhism denies the existence of a personal God.

> Any concept of God was beyond man's grasp and since Buddhism was a practical approach to life, why not deal with practical things? India, where Buddhism was born, had so many Hindu gods that no one could number them. They were often made in the image of men, but Buddhism was made in the image of concepts, great concepts about life and how life should be lived. If the truth were known, you often tell yourself, Buddhism has no God in the Hindu or Christian sense, nor does it have a saviour or a messiah. It has the Buddha. And he was the Enlightened One, the Shower-of-the Way (Marcus Bach, *Had You Been Born in Another Faith*, Englewood Cliffs, NJ: Prentice-Hall, 1961, p. 47).

There are those who deify the Buddha but along with him they worship other gods. The Scriptures make it clear that not only does a personal God exist, but He is to be the only object of worship. "'You are My witnesses,' declares the Lord, 'And My servant whom I have chosen, in order that you may know and believe Me, and understand that I am He. Before Me there was no God formed, and there will be none after Me'" (Isaiah 43:10 NASB). "Thus says the Lord, the King of Israel and His Redeemer, the Lord of hosts: 'I am the first and I am the last, and there is no God besides Me'" (Isaiah 44:6 NASB). "'I am the Lord your God, who brought you out of the land of Egypt, out of the house of slavery. You shall have no other gods before Me'" (Exodus 20:2, 3 NASB). "Then Jesus said to him, 'Begone, Satan! For it is written, "You shall worship the Lord your God, and serve Him only"'" (Matthew 4:10 NASB). "Jesus therefore said to them again, 'Truly, truly, I say to you, I am the door of the sheep. All who came before Me are thieves and robbers; but the sheep did not hear them. I am the door; if anyone enters through Me, he shall be saved and shall go in and out, and find pasture'" (John 10:7-9 NASB).

There is no such thing in Buddhism as sin against a supreme being. In Christianity sin is ultimately against God although sinful actions also affect man and his world. The Bible makes it clear, "against thee, thee only, I have sinned, and done what is evil in thy sight" (Psalm 51:4, NASB).

Accordingly man needs a savior to deliver him from his sins.

> The Bible teaches that Jesus Christ is that Savior and He offers the gift of salvation to all those who will believe, "The next day he saw Jesus coming to him, and said, 'Behold, the Lamb of God who takes away the sin of the world!'" (John 1:29 NASB). "And she will bear a Son; and you shall call His name Jesus, for it is he who will save His people from their sins" (Matthew 1:21 NASB). "For the wages of sin is death, but the free gift of God is eternal life in Christ Jesus our Lord" (Romans 6:23 NASB).

According to Buddhist belief, man is worthless, having only temporary existence. In Christianity man is of infinite worth, made in the image of God, and will exist eternally. Man's body is a hindrance to the Buddhist while to the Christian it is an instrument to glorify God.

> The Scriptures reveal, "Then God said, 'Let us make man in our image, according to our likeness; and let them rule over the fish of the sea and over the birds of the sky and over the cattle and over all the earth, and over every creeping thing that creeps on the earth'" (Genesis 1:26 NASB). "Or do you not know that your body is a temple of the Holy Spirit who is in you, whom you have from God, and that you are not your own?" (1 Corinthians 6:19 NASB).

Another problem with Buddhism is the many forms it takes. Consequently, there is a wide variety of belief in the different sects with much that is contradictory. John B. Noss makes an appropriate comment:

> "The rather odd fact is that there ultimately developed within Buddhism so many forms of religious organization, cultus and belief, such great changes even in the fundamentals of the faith, that one must say Buddhism as a whole is really,

like Hinduism, a family of religions rather than a single religion" (John B. Noss, *Man's Religions*, New York: Macmillan Company, 1969, p. 146).

With these and other differences, it can be seen readily that any harmonization of the two religions simply is not possible.

Buddhistic Terms

AN-ATTA — Literally, "not self." A concept in Theravada Buddhism denying the permanent existence of self as contained by physical and mental attributes.

BHIKKHU — A Buddhist monk who wanders about depending upon others for his basic necessities.

BODHI — A Buddhist term for the wisdom by which one attains enlightenment.

BODHISATTVA — In Mahayana Buddhism, one who postpones attaining nirvana in order to help others achieve this goal. In Theravada Buddhism, it is one who is on the way to becoming a Buddha. Gautama was called a Bodhisattva before he attained enlightenment.

BUDDHA — "The enlightened one." This title was given to Siddhartha Gautama, the founder of Buddhism, upon his enlightenment. Likewise, a person can attain this position through following the fourfold path to enlightenment.

BUDDHISM — The religion based upon the teachings of the Buddha (Siddhartha Gautama). The Buddha's main teaching revolved around the causes for human suffering and the way to salvation from this suffering could be achieved. The two main branches of Buddhism are called Mahayana and Theravada or Hinayana.

DALAI LAMA — The title of the head of the hierarchal system of Tibetan Buddhism. Worshipped as the reincarnation of Bodhisattva Chenresi.

DHAMMA — The teachings of the Buddha. Related to the Sanskrit *Dharma*, or virtuous principles.

DUKKHA — Suffering, which is rooted in desire and attachment.

GOHONZON — A small black wooden box used as an

object of religious devotion, an altar, in Nichiren Shoshu Buddhism.

HEART SUTRA—One of the most important scriptures to Zen Buddhists.

KOAN—A verbal puzzle in Zen Buddhism which aids the pupil in loosing himself from this world and moving toward enlightenment.

MAHAYANA—The form of Buddhism prevalent in China, Japan, Korea and Vietnam. Literally translated, means "the great vehicle."

MAYA—In Buddhism, the mother of Siddhartha Gautama (the Buddha). (See under *Hindu Terms* for additional meanings.)

NIRVANA—A difficult, if not impossible, word to define. In Buddhism, it is basically a blissful spiritual condition where the heart extinguishes passion, hatred and delusion. It is the highest spiritual plane one person can attain.

PITAKA—Literally, "basket." Refers to the "three baskets" (Tri-pitaka) of sacred Buddhist writings.

PURE LAND—Refers to a teaching in the Lotus Sutra which emphasizes faith in the Buddha of immeasurable light (Buddha Amitabha) and the goal of rebirth in his heaven of the pure land. Emphasizes easy attainment of nirvana. There are also Chinese and Japanese Pure Land sects.

PURE LAND BUDDHISM—A sect that bases its faith in the Amida Buddha (the Buddha of the infinite light) as its saviour who will lead his followers into a celestial paradise. Salvation is achieved by repeating Amida's name (the Nembutsu).

SAMSARA—The cycle of birth, suffering, death and rebirth.

SANGHA—The Buddhist monastic order literally translated as "group" or "community." May be the oldest order in Buddhism.

SATORI—The term for enlightenment in Zen Buddhism.

SOKA GOKKAI—The Creative-Value Study Society. The modern revival of a thirteenth century Buddhist sect, Nichiren Shoshu.

STUPAS—Originally, burial mounds, now used as relic chambers or memorials, especially of the Buddha.

THERAVADA—Literally the "teachings of the elders." The form of Buddhism that arose early among Buddha's disciples. Also called Hinayana Buddhism. Prevails in Southeast Asia.

TIBETAN BUDDHISM (LAMAISM)—A sect of Buddhism that began in Tibet in the seventh century A.D. It combined Buddhist principles with the occult religion of Tibet, producing Lamaism. The priests are all called Lamas and at the head is the Dalai Lama, a man who is worshipped as the reincarnated Bodhisattva Chenresi (Avalokita).

TRIPITAKA—See Pitaka.

TRUE SECT OF THE PURE LAND—A sect emphasizing the teachings of Pure Land (see above entry), founded in the thirteenth century by Shinran. Today it is the largest of any Buddhist sect in Japan.

VINAYA—The first of the three parts of the Pitaka, or scriptures of Buddhism, containing the rules of discipline of the Buddhist monastic order.

ZAREN—Zen meditation, concentrating on a problem or koan (see below).

Buddhism Bibliography

Agency for Cultural Affairs, *Japanese Religion: A Survey*, Tokyo, New York, and San Francisco: Kodansha International Ltd., 1972, 1981.

Bach, Marcus, *Had You Been Born in Another Faith*, Englewood Cliffs, NJ: Prentice-Hall, 1961.

Burtt, E. A., ed., *The Teachings of the Compassionate Buddha*, New York: New American Library, 1955.

Conze, Edward, *A Short History of Buddhism*, London: George Allen and Unwin Ltd., 1980.

Conze, Edward, et. al, *Buddhist Texts Through the Ages*, New York: Philosophical Library, 1954.

David-Neel, Alexandra, *Buddhism: Its Doctrines and Its Methods*, New York: St. Martin's Press, 1977.

Humphreys, Christmas, *Buddhism*, London: Penguin Books, 1951.

Martin, Walter, ed., *The New Cults*, Santa Ana, CA: Vision House Publishers Inc., 1980.

Noss, John B., *Man's Religions*, New York: MacMillan Company, 1969.

Offner, Clark B. in *The World's Religions*, Sir Norman Anderson, ed., Grand Rapids, MI: William B. Eerdmans Publishing Company, 1976.

Rice, Edward, *Eastern Definitions*, New York: Doubleday, 1980.

Robinson, Richard, trans., *Chinese Buddhist Verse*, London: Greenwood Publ., 1954.

Ross, Nancy Wilson, *Buddhism: A Way of Thought*, New York, Alfred A. Knopf, Inc., 1980.

Seeger, Elizabeth, *Eastern Religions*, New York: Crowell, 1973.

Smith, Huston, *The Religions of Man*, New York: Harper and Row, 1958.

Swearer, Donald K., *Buddhism*, Niles, IL: Argus Communications, 1977.

Confucianism

Confucianism, a religion of optimistic humanism, has had a monumental impact upon the life, social structure and political philosophy of China. The founding of the religion goes back to one man, known as Confucius, born a half-millenium before Christ.

History

The Life of Confucius

Although Confucius occupies a hallowed place in Chinese tradition, little is verifiable about his life. The best source available is *The Analects*, the collection of his sayings made by his followers. Long after his death much biographical detail on his life surfaced, but most of this material is of questionable historical value. However, there are some basic facts that can be accepted reasonably to give an outline of his life.

Confucius was born Chiu King, the youngest of 11 children, about 550 B.C., in the principality of Lu, which is located in present-day Shantung. He was a contemporary of the Buddha (although they probably never met) and lived immediately before Socrates and Plato. Nothing is known for certain concerning his ancestors except the fact that his surroundings were humble.

As he himself revealed: "When I was young I was without rank and in humble circumstances." His father died soon after his birth, leaving his upbringing to his mother. During his youth Confucius participated in a variety of activities, including hunting and fishing; but, "On reaching the age of 15, I bent my mind to learning."

He held a minor government post as a collector of taxes before he reached the age of 20. It was at this time that Confucius married. However, his marriage was short-lived, ending in divorce; but he did produce a son and a daughter from his unsuccessful marriage. He became a teacher in his early twenties, and that proved to be his calling in life.

His ability as a teacher became apparent and his fame spread rapidly, attracting a strong core of disciples. Many were attracted by his wisdom. He believed that society would not be changed unless he occupied a public office where he could put his theories into practice.

Confucius held minor posts until age 50, when he became a high official in Lu. His moral reforms achieved an immediate success, but he soon had a falling out with his superiors and subsequently resigned his post. Confucius spent the next 13 years wandering from state to state, attempting to implement his political and social reforms. He devoted the last five years of his life to writing and editing what have become Confucian classics.

He died in Chüfou, Shantung, in 479 B.C., having established himself as the most important teacher in Chinese culture. His disciples referred to him as King Fu-tzu or Kung the Master, which has been latinized into Confucius.

China Before Confucius

It is important to understand life in China at the time of Confucius in order to develop a better appreciation of the reforms he was attempting to institute. The age in which Confucius lived was characterized by social anarchy. Huston Smith gives insight into the condition of China during this difficult period:

> By Confucius' day, however, the interminable warfare had degenerated a long way from this code of chivalrous honor toward the undiluted horror of the Period of the Warring States. The horror reached its height in the century following Confucius' death. The chariot, arm of the tournament, gave

way to the cavalry with its surprise attacks and sudden raids. Instead of nobly holding their prisoners for ransom, conquerors put them to death in mass executions. Soldiers were paid upon presenting the severed heads of their enemies. Whole populations unlucky enough to be captured were beheaded, including women, children, and the aged. We read of mass slaughters of 60,000, 80,000, 82,000, and even 400,000. There are accounts of the conquered being thrown into boiling caldrons and their relatives forced to drink the human soup (Huston Smith, *The Religions of Man*, New York: Harper and Row, 1965, p. 166).

It is easy to see how the need arose for someone like Confucius to provide answers for how the people could live together harmoniously. Although the conduct of Chinese officials was exceedingly corrupt, Confucius believed the situation was not hopeless, for the general population had not reached the point of total corruption.

Confucius believed China could be saved if the people would seek for the good of others, a practice of their ancestors. The role Confucius would play was not as a savior or messiah but as one who would put the people back in touch with the ancients: "I transmit but do not create. I believe in and love the ancients. I venture to compare myself to our old P'eng (an ancient official who liked to tell stories)."

The Veneration of Confucius

Like many great religious leaders, Confucius was eventually deified by his followers. The following chart traces the progress which led to his ultimate deification:

B.C.
195   The Emperor of China offered animal sacrifice at the tomb of Confucius.

A.D.
1   He was given the imperial title "Duke Ni, All-complete and Illustrious."

57   Regular sacrifice to Confucius was ordered at the imperial and provincial colleges.

89   He was raised to the higher imperial rank of "Earl."

267   More elaborate animal sacrifices to Confucius were decreed four times yearly.

492	He was canonized as "The Venerable, the Accomplished Sage."
555	Separate temples for the worship of Confucius were ordered at the capital of every prefecture in China.
740	The statue of Confucius was moved from the side to the center of the Imperial College, to stand with the historic kings of China.
1068-1086	Confucius was raised to the full rank of Emperor.
1906	December 31. An Imperial Rescript raised him to the rank of Co-assessor with the deities Heaven and Earth.
1914	The worship of Confucius was continued by the first President of the Republic of China, Yuan Shi Kai (Robert E. Hume, *The World's Living Religions*, New York: Charles Scribner's Sons, rev. ed., 1959, pp. 117, 118).

The Life of Mencius

One of the central figures in Confucianism is Meng-tzu (Latinized into Mencius) who became second only to Confucius in the history of Confucian thought. Mencius, born in the state of Ch'i in 371 B.C., studied with a disciple of Confucius' grandson, Tzu-ssu.

Like his master, Mencius spent most of his life traveling from state to state, seeking those in leadership who would adopt the teachings of Confucius. The feudal order in China had become worse than in the days of Confucius, and the attempts of Mencius to reverse this trend were of no avail.

Mencius, rejected by the politicians of his day, turned to teaching and developing Confucian thought. Among his accomplishments was the clarification of a question that Confucius left ambiguous: the basic nature of man. Mencius taught that man is basically good. This is still a basic presupposition of Confucian thought.

In his classic example, Mencius compared the potentiality of the goodness of man to the natural flow of water. Though water naturally flows downward, it can be made to flow uphill or splashed above one's head, but only as a result of external force. Likewise man's nature is basically good but can be forced into bad ways through external pressure.

This teaching, which is diametrically opposed to the biblical doctrine of original and universal sin, has made the proclamation of the Gospel that much more difficult among the people in China who accept the ideas of Mencius concerning the nature of man.

Confucius and Lao-tzu

There are reports, perhaps untrue, that Confucius met with Lao-tzu (var. sp.: Lao-tze), the founder of Taoism. Confucius had heard about the old archivist with strange philosophical beliefs and decided to investigate. The meeting was anything but amiable, however. Confucius, still a young man, had become famous because of his teachings and wisdom, and Lao-tzu was annoyed with him.

Joseph Gaer records what is believed to have taken place:

Confucius had prepared a number of questions he wished to ask of Lao-tze concerning his doctrines. But before he could even begin on the topic, Lao-tze questioned Confucius about his interests.

Confucius replied that he was interested in the history of the Ancients, especially as recorded in *The Book of Annals (Shu K'ing)*.

"The men of whom you speak are long since dead and their bones are turned to ashes in their graves." Lao-tze interrupted.

Their talk continued, with Lao-tze asking the questions and Confucius answering them deferentially and politely. It was his belief, Confucius explained, that man is by nature good, and that knowledge can keep him good.

"But why study the Ancients?" Lao-tze asked impatiently.

Confucius tried to explain his belief that new knowledge must be based upon old knowledge.

Lao-tze interrupted him, saying: "Put away your polite airs and your vain display of fine robes. The wise man does not display his treasure to those he does not know. And he cannot learn justice from the Ancients."

"Why not?" asked Confucius.

"It is not bathing that makes the pigeon white," was Lao-tze's reply. And he abruptly ended the interview (Joseph Gaer, *What the Great Religions Believe*, New York: Dodd, Mead, and Company, 1963, p. 76).

Whether or not this meeting occured, the account amply illustrates the difference between the two men and the religions which proceeded from them.

The Sources of Confucianism

During his teaching career Confucius collected ancient manuscripts which he edited and on which he wrote commentaries. He arranged these manuscripts into four books to which he also added a fifth book of his own. These works are known as the *Five Classics*.

The Five Classics

The Five Classics as we have them today have gone through much editing and alteration by Confucius' disciples, yet there is much in them that can be considered the work of Confucius. *The Five Classics* are:

1. *The Book of Changes (I Ching)* The I Ching is a collection of eight triagrams and 64 hexagrams which consist solely of broken and unbroken lines. These lines were supposed to have great meaning if the key were discovered.

2. *The Book of Annals (Shu K'ing)* This is a work of the history of the five preceding dynasties. The example of the ancients was crucial to Confucius' understanding of how the superior man should behave.

3. *The Book of Poetry (Shih Ching)* The book of ancient poetry was assembled by Confucius because he believed the reading of poetry would aid in making a man virtuous.

4. *The Book of Ceremonies (Li Chi)* This work taught the superior man to act in the right or traditional way. Again Confucius stressed doing things in the same way as the ancients.

5. *The Annals of Spring and Autumn (Ch'un Ch'iu)* This book, supposedly written by Confucius, gave a commentary on the events of the state of Lu at Confucius' time.

The Teachings of Confucius

None of these works contain the unique teaching of Confucius but are rather an anthology of works he collected and from which he taught. Confucius' own teachings have come down to us from four books written by his disciples. They include:

1. *The Analects.* This is the most important source we have on Confucius. *The Analects* are sayings of both Confucius and his disciples.

2. *The Great Learning.* This work which deals with the education and training of a gentleman comes not from the hand of Confucius but rather from a later period (about 250 B.C.).

3. *The Doctrine of the Mean.* This work deals with the relationship of human nature to the order of the universe. Authorship is uncertain (part of it may be attributed to Confucius' grandson Tzu-Ssu), but it does not come from Confucius.

4. *The Book of Mencius.* Mencius wrote the first exposition of Confucian thought about 300 B.C. by collecting earlier teachings and attempting to put them down systematically. This work, which has had great influence and gives an idealistic view of life, stresses the goodness of human nature.

The Doctrines of Confucianism

Ancestor Worship

A common feature of Chinese religion prevalent at Confucius' time was the veneration of ancestors. Ancestor worship is the veneration of the spirits of the dead by their living relatives. Supposedly the continued existence of the ancestors in spirit is dependent upon the attention given them by their living relatives. It is also believed that the ancestors can control the fortunes of their families.

If the family provides for the ancestors' needs, then the ancestors will in turn cause good things to happen to their relatives. However, if the ancestors are neglected, it is believed that all sorts of evil can fall upon the living. Consequently, the living sometimes live in fear of the dead. Richard C. Bush expands upon this thought:

The veneration of ancestors by royal families and common people alike reveals several reasons for ancestor worship. People wanted their ancestors to be able to live beyond the grave in a manner similar to their life-style on earth; hence the living attempted to provide whatever would be necessary. A secondary motive lurks in the background: if not provided with the food and weapons and utensils needed to survive in the life beyond, those ancestors might return as ghosts and cause trouble for the living. To this day people celebrate a Festival of the Hungry Ghosts, placing food and wine in front of their homes to satisfy those ancestral spirits or ghosts whose descendants have not cared for them and who therefore may wander back to old haunts. A third motive is to inform the ancestors of what is going on at the present time, hopefully in such a way that the ancestral spirits may be assured that all is well and therefore may rest in peace. Finally, ancestor worship expresses the hope that ancestors will bless the living with children, prosperity, and harmony, and all that is most worthwhile (Richard C. Bush, *The Story of Religion in China*, Niles, IL: Argus Communications, 1977, p. 2).

Filial Piety

A concept that was entrenched in China long before the time of Confucius is that of filial piety (*Hsaio*) which can be described as devotion and obedience by the younger members of the family to the elders. This was particularly the case of son to father. This loyalty and devotion to the family was the top priority in Chinese life. Such duty to the family, particularly devotion to the elders, was continued throughout one's life.

This was expressed in *The Classic of Filial Piety:* "The services of love and reverence to parents when alive, and those of grief and sorrow to them when dead—these completely discharge the fundamental duty of living men" (Max Mueller, ed., *Sacred Books of the East*, Krishna Press, 1879-1910, Vol. III, p. 448).

Confucius stressed this concept in his teachings, and it was well received by the Chinese people, both then and now. In *The Analects*, Confucius said:

The master said, "A young man should be a good son at home and an obedient young man abroad, sparing of speech but trustworthy in what he says, and should love the multitude at large but cultivate the friendship of his fellow men" (I:6).

Meng Wu Po asked about being filial. The master said, "Give your father and mother no other cause for anxiety than illness" (II:6).

Tzu-yu asked about being filial. The master said, "Nowadays for a man to be filial means no more than that he is able to provide his parents with food. Even hounds and horses are in some way provided with food. If a man shows no reverence, where is the difference?" (II:2).

Doctrinal Principles

Confucianism's doctrines can be summarized by six key terms or ways. *Jen* is the golden rule; *Chun-tzu* the gentleman; *Cheng-ming* is the role-player; *Te* is virtuous power; *Li* is the standard of conduct; and *Wen* encompasses the arts of peace. A brief discussion of the six principles reveals the basic doctrinal structure of Confucianism.

1. *Jen.* *Jen* has the idea of humaneness, goodness, benevolence or man-to-manness. *Jen* is the golden rule, the rule of reciprocity; that is to say, do not do anything to others that you would not have them do to you.

   "Tzu-Kung asked, 'Is there a single word which can be a guide to conduct throughout one's life?' The master said, 'It is perhaps the word "Shu." Do not impose on others what you yourself do not desire'" (Confucius, *The Analects*, XV:24).

   This is the highest virtue according to the Confucian way of life; if this principle could be put into practice, then mankind would achieve peace and harmony.

2. *Chun-tzu.* *Chun-tzu* can be translated variously as the gentleman, true manhood, the superior man, and man-at-his-best. The teachings of Confucius were aimed toward the gentleman, the man of virtue.

   Huston Smith observes, "If *Jen* is the ideal relationship between human beings, *Chun-tzu* refers to the ideal term of such relations" (Smith, *op. cit.*, p. 180). Confucius had this to say about the gentleman:

   (Confucius:) He who in this world can practice five things may indeed be considered man-at-his-best.

   What are they?

   Humility, magnanimity, sincerity, diligence, and graciousness. If you are humble, you will not be laughed at. If you are magnanimous, you will attract many to your side. If you are sincere, people will trust you. If you are gracious, you will get along well with your subordinates (James R. Ware, trans., *The Sayings of Confucius*, New York: New American Library, 1955, p. 110).

   It is this type of man who can transform society into the peaceful state it was meant to be.

3. *Cheng-ming*. Another important concept according to Confucius was *Cheng-ming*, or the rectification of names. For a society to be properly ordered, Confucius believed everyone must act his proper part. Consequently, a king should act like a king, a gentleman like a gentleman, etc.

    Confucius said, "Duke Ching of Ch'i asked Confucius about government. Confucius answered, 'Let the ruler be a ruler, the subject a subject, the father a father, the son a son....'" (*The Analects*, XII:11).

    He said elsewhere, "Tzu-lu said, 'If the Lord of Wei left the administration (*cheng*) of his state to you, what would you put first?' The master said, 'If something has to be put first, it is perhaps the rectification of names'" (*The Analects*, XIII:3).

4. *Te*. The word *te* literally means "power," but the concept has a far wider meaning. The power needed to rule, according to Confucius, consists of more than mere physical might. It is necessary that the leaders be men of virtue who can inspire their subjects to obedience through example. This concept had been lost during Confucius' time with the prevailing attitude being that physical might was the only proper way to order a society.

    Confucius looked back at history to the sages of the past, Yao and Shun, along with the founders of the Chou dynasty, as examples of such virtuous rule. If the rulers would follow the example of the past, then the people would rally around the virtuous example.

5. *Li*. One of the key words used by Confucius is *li*. The term has a variety of meanings, depending upon the context. It can mean propriety, reverence, courtesy, ritual or the ideal standard of conduct. In the Book of Ceremonies (*The Li Chi*), the concept of *li* is discussed:

    Duke Ai asked Confucius, "What is this great *li*? Why is it that you talk about *li* as though it were such an important thing?"

    Confucius replied, "Your humble servant is really not worthy to understand *li*."

    "But you constantly speak about it," said Duke Ai.

    Confucius: "What I have learned is this, that of all the things that people live by, *li* is the greatest. Without *li*, we do not know how to conduct a proper worship of the spirits of the universe; or how to establish the proper status of the king and the ministers, the ruler and the ruled, and the elders and the juniors; or how to establish the moral relationships between the sexes; between parents and children, and between brothers; or how to distinguish the different degrees of relationships in the family. That is why a gentleman holds *li* in such high regard" (Lin Yutang, *The Wisdom of Confucius*, New York: Random House, 1938, *Li Chi* XXVII, p. 216).

6. *Wen.* The concept of *Wen* refers to the arts of peace, which Confucius held in high esteem. These include music, poetry and art. Confucius felt that these arts of peace, which came from the earlier Chou period, were symbols of virtue that should be manifest throughout society.

Confucius condemned the culture of his day because he believed it lacked any inherent virtue. He had this to say:

> The master said, "Surely when one says, 'The rites, the rites,' it is not enough merely to mean presents of jade and silk. Surely when one says 'music, music,' it is not enough merely to mean bells and drums...."
> The master said, "What can a man do with the rites who is not benevolent? What can a man do with music who is not benevolent?" (*The Analects*, XVII:11, III:3).

Therefore, he who rejected the arts of peace was rejecting the virtuous ways of man and heaven.

Ethical Doctrines

The *Book of Analects* (*Lun Yu*) contains the sayings of Confucius which present his ethical principles. The following excerpts are from *The Analects* and give an example of the teachings of Confucius:

> Men of superior minds busy themselves first getting at the root of things; when they succeed, the right course is open to them.
>
> One excellent way to practice the rules of propriety is to be natural.
>
> When truth and right go hand in hand, a statement will bear repetition.
>
> Sorrow not because men do not know you; but sorrow that you do not know men.
>
> To govern simply by statute and to maintain order by means of penalties is to render the people evasive and devoid of a sense of shame.
>
> If you observe what people take into their hands, observe

the motives, note what gives them satisfaction; then will they be able to conceal from you what they are?

When you know a thing, maintain you know it; when you do not, acknowledge it. This is the characteristic of knowledge.

Let the leader of men promote those who have ability, and instruct those who have it not, and they will be willing to be led.

To see what is right and not to do it, that is cowardice.

The superior man is not contentious. He contends only as in competitions of archery; and when he wins he will present his cup to his competitor.

A man without charity in his heart, what has he to do with ceremonies? A man without charity in his heart, what has he to do with music?

He who has sinned against Heaven has none other to whom his prayer may be addressed.

Tell me, is there anyone who is able for one whole day to apply the energy of his mind to virtue? It may be that there are such, but I have never met with one.

If we may learn what is right in the morning, we should be content to die in the evening.

The scholar who is intent upon learning the truth, yet is ashamed of his poor clothes and food, is not worthy to be discoursed with.

The superior man thinks of his character; the inferior man thinks of his position; the former thinks of the penalties for error, and the latter, of favors.

One should not be greatly concerned at not being in office, but rather about the requirements in one's self for that office. Nor should one be greatly concerned at being unknown, but rather with being worthy to be known.

The superior man seeks what is right, the inferior one what is profitable.

The superior man is slow to promise, prompt to fulfill.

Virtue dwells not in solitude; she must have neighbors.

In my first dealings with a man, I listen to his avowals and trust his conduct; after that I listen to his avowals and watch his conduct.

These are the four essential qualities of the superior man: he is humble, he is deferential to superiors, he is generously kind, and he is always just.

Those who are willing to forget old grievances will gradually do away with resentment.

I have not yet seen the man who can see his errors so as in a day to accuse himself.

Where plain naturalness is more in evidence than fine manners, we have the country man; where fine manners are more in evidence than plain naturalness, we have the townsman; where the two are equally blended we have the ideal man.

Better than the one who knows what is right is he who loves what is right.

To prize the effort above the prize, that is virtue.

What you find in me is a quiet brooder and memorizer, a student never satiated with learning, an unwearied monitor to others.

These things weigh heavily upon my mind: failure to improve in the virtues, failure in discussion of what is learned, inability to walk always according to the knowledge of what is right and just, inability to reform what has been amiss.

Fix your mind on truth; hold firm to virtue; rely upon loving-kindness; and find your recreation in the arts.

With coarse food to eat, water to drink, and a bent arm for a pillow, happiness may still be found.

Let there be three men walking together, and in them I will be sure to find my instructors. For what is good in them I will follow; and what is not good I will try to modify.

Sift out the good from the many things you hear, and follow them; sift out the good from the many things you see and remember them.

Without a sense of proportion, courtesy becomes oppressive; calmness becomes bashfulness; valor becomes disorderliness; and candor becomes rudeness.

Even if a person were adorned with the gift of the Duke of Chau, if he is proud and avaricious, all his other qualities are not really worth looking at.

Learn as if you could never overtake your subject, yet as if apprehensive of losing it.

When you have erred, be not afraid to correct yourself.

It is easier to carry off the chief commander of an army than to rob one poor fellow of his will.

We know so little about life, how can we then know about death?

If a man can subdue his selfishness for one full day, everyone will call him good.

When you leave your house, go out as if to meet an important guest.

Do not set before others what you yourself do not like.

The essentials of good government are: a sufficiency of food, a sufficiency of arms, and the confidence of the people. If forced to give up one of these, give up arms; and if forced to give up two, give up food. Death has been the portion of all men from of old; but without the people's trust, nothing can endure.

A tiger's or a leopard's skin might be a dog's or a sheep's when stripped of its hair.

Hold fast to what is good and the people will be good. The virtue of the good man is as the wind; and that of the bad man, as the grass. When the wind blows, the grass must bend.

Knowledge of man, that is wisdom.

The superior man feels reserved in matters which he does not understand.

Let the leader show rectitude in his personal character, and things will go well even without directions from him.

Do not wish for speedy results nor trivial advantages; speedy results will not be far-reaching; trivial advantages will matter only in trivial affairs.

The superior man will be agreeable even when he disagrees; the inferior man will be disagreeable even when he agrees.

Confucius was asked, "Is a good man one who is liked by everybody?" He answered, "No." "Is it one who is disliked by everybody?" He answered, "No. He is liked by all the good people and disliked by the bad."

In a country of good government, the people speak out boldly and act boldly.

Good men speak good words, but not all who speak good words are good. Good men are courageous, but not all courageous men are good.

The Supernatural

Confucianism is not a religion in the sense of man relating to the Almighty but is rather an ethical system teaching man how to get along with his fellow man. However, Confucius did make some comments on the supernatural which give insight into how he viewed life, death, heaven, etc. He once said, "Absorption in the study of the supernatural is most harmful" (Lionel Giles, *Sayings of Confucius, Wisdom of the East Series*, London: John Murray Publ., 1917, II:16, 94). When asked about the subject of death, he had this to say, "Chi-lu asked how the spirits of the dead and the gods should be served. The master said, 'You are not able to serve man. How can you serve the spirits?' 'May I ask about death?' 'You do not understand even life. How can you understand death?'" (Confucius, *The Analects*, D. C. Lau, trans., London: Penguin Books, 1979, Book XI, 12).

John B. Noss comments, "His position in matters of faith was this: whatever seemed contrary to common sense in popular tradition, and whatever did not serve any discoverable social purpose, he regarded coldly" (John B. Noss, *Man's Religions*, New York: MacMillan Company, 1969, p. 291).

Confucius did, however, feel that heaven was on his side in the ethical teachings that he espoused, as can be observed by the following comment:

"The master said, 'At fifteen I set my heart on learning; at thirty I took my stand; at forty I came to be free from doubts; at fifty I understood the decree of heaven; at sixty my ear was attuned; at seventy I followed my heart's desire without overstepping the line'" (*The Analects*, II:5).

Is Confucianism a Religion?

Since Confucianism deals primarily with moral conduct and the ordering of society, it is often categorized as an ethical system rather than a religion. Although Confucianism deals solely with life here on earth rather than the afterlife, it does take into consideration mankind's ultimate concerns.

One must remember the outlook of the people during the time of Confucius. Deceased ancestors were thought to exercise power over the living, sacrifice to heaven was a common occurrence, and the practice of augury, or observing the signs from heaven (thunder, lightning, the flight of birds, etc.), all were prevalent. Huston Smith makes an appropriate comment:

In each of these three great features of early Chinese religion—its sense of continuity with the ancestors, its sacrifice, and its augury—there was a common emphasis. The emphasis was on Heaven instead of Earth. To understand the total dimensions of Confucianism as a religion, it is important to see Confucius (a) shifting the emphasis from Heaven to Earth (b) without dropping Heaven out of the picture entirely (Huston Smith, *op. cit.*, p. 189).

The emphasis in Confucianism was on the earthly, not the heavenly; but heaven and its doings were assumed to be real rather than imaginary. Since Confucianism gradually assumed control over all of one's life, and it was the presupposition from which all action was decided, it necessarily permeated Chinese religious thought, belief and practice as well.

The Impact of Confucianism

The impact Confucianism has had on China can hardly be over-estimated. Huston Smith observes:

History to date affords no clearer support for this thesis than the work of Confucius. For over two thousand years his teachings have profoundly affected a quarter of the population of this globe. Their advance reads like a success story of the spirit. During the Han Dynasty (206 B.C.-A.D.-20), Confucianism became, in effect, China's state religion. In 130 B.C. it was made the basic discipline for the training of government officials, a pattern which continued in the main until the establishment of the Republic in 1912. In 59 A.D. sacrifices were ordered for Confucius in all urban schools, and in the seventh and eighth centuries temples were erected in every prefecture of the empire as shrines to him and his principal disciples. To the second half of the twelfth century his *The Analects* remained one of the classics. But in the Sung Dynasty it became not merely a school book but the school book, the basis of all education. In 1934 his birthday was proclaimed a national holiday (*Ibid.*, p. 192).

Marcus Bach in a similar way relates:

One thing that the Communist regime will never be able to do is to get Confucius out of China. Some say it has not been tried. Others contend there is no use trying. China's...people know Confucius as well as America's millions know the Christ. We do not have a state religion, but we are predominantly Christian. China does not have a state religion, but it is predominantly Confucian (Marcus Bach, *Major Religons of the World*, Nashville: Abingdon, 1970, p. 81).

Confucianism and Christianity

The ethical system taught by Confucius has much to commend it, for virtue is something to desire highly. However, the ethical philosophy Confucius espoused was one of self-effort, leaving no room or need for God.

Confucius taught that man can do it all by himself if he only follows the way of the ancients, while Christianity teaches that man does not have the capacity to save himself but is in desperate need of a savior. Confucius also hinted that human nature was basically good. This thought was developed by later Confucian teachers and became a cardinal belief of Confucianism.

The Bible, on the other hand, teaches that man is basically sinful and left to himself is completely incapable of performing ultimate good. Contrast what the Bible says about human nature and the need of a savior against Confucianism.

"The heart is more deceitful than all else and is desperately sick; Who can understand it?" (Jeremiah 17:9, NASB). "For all have sinned and fall short of the glory of God" (Romans 3:23, NASB). "For by grace you have been saved through faith; and that not of yourselves, it is the gift of God: not as a result of works, that no one should boast" (Ephesians 2:8, 9, NASB). "He saved us, not on the basis of deeds which we have done in righteousness, but according to His mercy, by the washing of regeneration and renewing by the Holy Spirit" (Titus 3:5, NASB).

Since Confucianism lacks any emphasis upon the supernatural, this religious system must be rejected. It must be remembered that Confucius taught an ethical philosophy that later germinated into a popular religion, though Confucius had no idea that his teachings would become the state religion in China. Nevertheless, Confucianism as a religious system is opposed to the teachings of Christianity and must be rejected summarily by Christians.

Confucianistic Terms

ANALECTS, THE—One of the *Four Books* containing the

sayings of Confucius. *The Analects* are considered the best source of determining the sayings and wisdom of Confucius.

ANCESTOR WORSHIP—the Chinese practice of worshipping the spirits of their dead relatives in order to appease them from causing trouble with the living.

CHENG MENG—The concept of rectification of names, meaning that one should act in accordance with his position in life (king as a king, father as a father, etc.).

CHUN-TZU—"Man-at-his best," the superior man. The type of man, according to Confucius, who could transform society into a peaceful state.

CONFUCIUS—"Kung the Master," the title for Chiu King, the founder of Confucianism.

FENG SHUI—The Chinese name for geomancy, a branch of divination to determine appropriate sights for houses or graves.

FILIAL PIETY—The Chinese practice of loyalty and devotion by the younger members of the family to their elders.

FIVE CLASSICS—Along with the *Four Books*, the Five Classics are the authoritative writings of Confucianism. The Five Classics were collected and edited by Confucius. They include: *The Book of Changes, The Book of Annals, The Book of Poetry, The Book of Ceremonies*, and *The Annals of Spring and Autumn*.

FOUR BOOKS—The Four Books are a collection of the teachings and sayings of Confucius. They include: *The Analects, The Great Learning, The Doctrine of the Mean, The Book of Mencius*.

JEN—The golden rule in Confucianism, "Do not do to others what you would not have them do to you."

LI—The concept denoting the ideal standard of conduct.

MANDATE OF HEAVEN—The authorization of power to Chinese emperors and kings believed traditionally to issue from heaven.

MENCIUS—A later disciple of Confucius who is credited with developing and systematizing Confucian thought.

TE—The virtuous power needed to properly rule the people.

WEN — The arts of peace, which include poetry, music, and art.

Confucianism Bibliography

Bach, Marcus, *Major Religions of the World*, Nashville: Abingdon, 1979.

Bush, Richard C., *The Story of Religion in China*, Niles, IL: Argus Communications, 1977.

Confucius, *The Analects*, D. C. Lau, trans., London: Penguin Books, 1979.

Gaer, Joseph, *What the Great Religions Believe*, New York: Dodd, Mead, and Company, 1963.

Giles, Lionel, *Sayings of Confucius*, *Wisdom of the East Series*, London: John Murray Publ., 1917.

Hume, Robert E., *The World's Living Religions*, New York: Charles Scribner's Sons, rev. ed., 1959.

Mueller, Max, ed., *Sacred Books of the East*, *Fifty Volumes*, London: Krishna Press, 1879-1910.

Noss, John B., *Man's Religions*, New York: MacMillan Company, 1969.

Smith, Huston, *The Religions of Man*, New York: Harper and Row, 1965.

Ware, James R., trans., *The Sayings of Confucius*, New York: New American Library, 1955.

Yutang, Lin, *The Wisdom of Confucius*, New York: Random House, 1938.

Taoism

At the same time Confucius' teachings were spreading through China, another religion was also having its beginning. In contrast to the humanistic, ethical teachings of Confucius, the mystical, enigmatic beliefs of Taoism (pronounced "Dowism") appeared. Behind this enigmatic religion is itself an enigmatic figure named Lao-tzu.

History

Lao-tzu, the Founder

Taoism has its roots in a shadowy figure named Lao-tzu, of whom little or nothing is verifiable. Many scholars feel that Lao-tzu never existed at all. His date of birth is uncertain, being put variously between 604 and 570 B.C. One legend said that he was never young but rather was born old with white hair, a long white beard and wrinkled skin.

Another story has him named Plum-Tree-Ears by his mother because he was born under the shadow of a plum tree and his ears were unusually long. However, he was known to the people as Lao-tzu, meaning "the old philosopher." He supposedly held an important post as curator of the imperial archives at Loyang, the capital city in the state of Ch'u.

His government position became tiresome, for Lao-tzu

disapproved of the tyranny of the rulers and the idea of government itself. Lao-tzu came to believe that men were meant to live simply without honors and without a fruitless search for knowledge. Consequently, he resigned his post and returned home.

Since his opinions had gathered unwanted students and disciples, Lao-tzu left his house to seek privacy from curiosity seekers. He bought a cart and a black ox and set out toward the border of the province, leaving corrupt society behind. However, at the crossing of the border the guard, his friend Yin-hsi, recognized him and would not allow him to pass.

Yin-hsi exhorted Lao-tzu, "You have always kept to yourself like a hermit and have never written down your teachings. Yet many know them. Now you wish to leave and retire beyond our borders. I will not let you cross until you have written down the essentials of your teachings."

Lao-tzu returned after three days with a small treatise entitled *The Tao Te King,* or *The Way and Its Power* (sometimes translated as *The Way and Moral Principle*). Then he mounted a water buffalo and rode off into the sunset, never to be heard of again. Another version of the story has the gatekeeper Yin-hsi begging Lao-tzu to take him with him after he read *The Tao Te King.* Whatever the case may be, the little book was left behind and became the basis for a new religion.

Lao-tzu, the Book

The Tao Te King, also known as the *Lao-tzu,* is a small book of approximately 5,500 words instructing rulers in the art of government. It teaches that the less government, the better, and that a ruler should lead by non-action.

Needless to say, no ruler in the history of China has taken the political section seriously. However, there is a philosophical side to *The Tao Te King* that has had enormous impact. The work teaches individuals how to endure life against the terrible calamities that were common in China. It advocates a low-key approach of non-ambition and staying in the background which will help one's odds of survival.

There is an ongoing debate as to when *The Tao Te King*

was composed. The traditionalist point of view has the work composed by Lao-tzu, a contemporary of Confucius, in the sixth century B.C. The basis for holding this traditional date is the biography of Lao-tzu in the *Shih-chi (Records of the Historian)* about 100 B.C.

The modernists view the work as having been formally compiled about 300 B.C. because of the similarity of style to works composed in that period. The historical setting, they argue, fits more with this turbulent era than with the earlier one claimed by the traditionalists, although the modernists do believe many of the sayings actually come from a much earlier time.

Chuang-tzu

Apart from Lao-tzu, the most important figure in Taoism is Chuang-tzu, a disciple of the famous Lao-tzu. Chuang-tzu was a prolific author living during the fourth century B.C. who wrote some 33 books. Chuang-tzu was a clever writer, popularizing the teachings of Lao-tzu as Mencius did with his master, Confucius.

The following excerpts from the writings of Chuang-tzu give insight into the philosophical side of Taoism which he helped popularize:

> Once I, Chuang Chou, dreamed that I was a butterfly and was happy as a butterfly...Suddenly I awoke, and there I was, visibly Chou. I do not know whether it was Chou dreaming that he was a butterfly or the butterfly dreaming it was Chou. Between Chou and the butterfly there must be some distinction. This is called the transformation of things (Wing-Tsit Chan, ed., *A Sourcebook in Chinese Philosophy*, Princeton, NJ: Princeton University Press, 1963, p. 190).

Upon hearing the news of the death of his wife, Chuang-tzu responded:

> When she died, how could I help being affected? But as I think the matter over, I realize that originally she had no life; and not only no life, she had no form; not only no form, she had no material force. In the limbo of existence and non-existence, there was transformation and the material force was evolved. The material force was transformed to become form, form was transformed to become life, and now birth has transformed to become death. This is like the rotation of the four seasons, spring, summer, fall, and winter. Now she

lies asleep in the great house (the universe). For me to go about weeping and wailing would be to show my ignorance of destiny. Therefore I desist (*Ibid.*, p. 209).

Taoist History Review

Robert E. Hume charts some of the highlights in the history of Taoism:

B.C.

212   Emperor Shi Huang Ti burned Confucian books, and established Taoism; sent naval expeditions to Fairy Islands to discover the herb of immortality.

A.D.

1   The leading Taoist in China endeavored to compound a pill of immortality.

156   Emperor Hwan of China first sacrificed to Lao-tze.

574-581   Emperor Wu arranged order of precedence, viz., Confucianism, first; Taoism, second; and Buddhism, third; but soon became disgusted with Taoism and Buddhism and ordered their abolition. The next emperor, Tsing, re-established both non-Confucian religions.

650-684   Lao-tze canonized as an emperor; his writings included among subjects for government examinations.

713-742   Emperor Kai Yuen distributed copies of the *Tao-Teh-King* throughout the empire; took a dose of Taoist "gold-stone" medicine; magicry increased.

825-827   Emperor Pao-li banished all Taoist doctors on account of their intrigues and pretensions away to the two southernmost provinces of China.

841-847   Emperor Wu Tsung ordered all Taoist and Buddhist monasteries and nunneries closed. Later he restored Taoism to imperial favor, and stigmatized Buddhism as "a foreign religion." Took Taoist medicine to etherealize his bones, so as to fly through the air like the fairies.

1661-1721   Emperor Kang Hsi ordered punishment not only of the Taoist quacks, but also of the patients; forbade Taoist assemblies and processions; endeavored to suppress the various Taoist sects.

1900   The Boxer Uprising originated in a sect of specially ardent Taoists who believed their bodies would be immune against foreigners' bullets, trusting the exact words of the founder: "When coming among solders, he need not fear arms and weapons..." (Robert E. Hume, *The World's Living Religions*, New York: Charles Scribner's Sons, rev. ed., 1959, pp. 147, 148).

The Teachings of Taoism

The Tao

In *The Tao Te King*, the central concept is that of the Tao. Finding the proper definition of the term is no easy task, for while the word "Tao" literally means "way" or "path," the concept goes far beyond that. The opening words of *The Tao Te King* express the thought that the Tao that can be understood is not the real Tao. The name that can be named is not the real name.

A famous Taoist saying is, "Those who know don't say and those who say don't know." It is a mysterious term beyond all our understanding, imagination and senses. Yet it is the way of ultimate reality, the ground of all existence. It is the way of the universe, the way by which one should order his life.

> The cosmic Tao is invisible, inaudible, unnamable, un-discussable, inexpressible (Max Mueller, ed., *Sacred Books of the East*, London: Krishna Press, 1879-1910, 40:68, 69).
>
> The perfect man is peaceful like the Tao (*Ibid.*, 39:192-193).
>
> The ideal condition is a by-gone utopian simplicity in a state of nature (*Ibid.*, 39:278).
>
> Vacancy, stillness, placidity, tastelessness, quietude, silence, non-action—this is the level of Heaven and Earth, and the perfection of the Tao (*Ibid.*, 39:331).

The question arises, how does one get his life in harmony with the Tao? If mankind's chief aim is to conform his existence to the way of the Tao, what must he do to accomplish this? *The Tao Te King* teaches this can be done by practicing the basic attitude of *Wu Wei*, which literally means inaction.

This principle calls for the avoidance of all aggressiveness by doing that which is natural and spontaneous. Mankind should live passively, avoiding all forms of stress and violence to properly commune with nature. In doing this, his life will flow with the Tao.

Yin and Yang

A concept that has been accepted in Confucianism, as well as philosophical and religious Taoism, is that of the *yin* and *yang*. Although all things emanate from the Tao, there are those elements that are contrary to each other, such as good and evil and life and death. The positive side is known as the "yang" and the negative side the "yin." These opposites can be expressed in the following manner:

Yang	Yin
Male	Female
Positive	Negative
Good	Evil
Light	Darkness
Life	Death
Summer	Winter
Active	Passive

These concepts are interdependent and find themselves as expressions of the Tao. The concept of yin and yang is used to explain the ebb and flow in both man and nature. According to Taoism, "to blend with the cycle (of the universe) without effort is to become one with the Tao and so find fulfillment" (Maurice Rawlings, *Life-Wish: Reincarnation: Reality or Hoax*, Nashville, TN: Thomas Nelson Inc., 1981).

A broader Chinese concept regarding yin and yang is that the harmonious life can be achieved with the proper interaction of these forces. Richard C. Bush expands this idea:

> An understanding of the world had emerged: there were powers from above associated with Heaven such as rain and sun, and powers of the earth below such as the fertility of the soil. It follows naturally that the forces of heaven and earth should be in a state of interaction and that all of life flows from this interaction. All people have observed this process in nature, have planted and harvested their crops accordingly, and therefore developed a rhythm of life. The ancient Chinese sensed beneath this rhythm the movement of two basic forces called yang and yin. Yang is above, male, light,

warm and aggressive; yin is below, female, dark, cold, and passive. Harmonious life is a complementary interaction of male and female, darkness and light. Rain and sun (yang) fall on the earth (yin) and crops grow. The passive yields to the aggressive but, by yielding, absorbs and overcomes. The result is a philosophy of continual change which is believed to explain the rise and fall of dynasties as well as the change from day to night and back to day again. The goal of this process is a harmony between ruler and subject, among the members of the family, and in society as a whole becomes the goal of life, both in ancient China and among many Chinese today (Richard C. Bush, *The Story of Religion in China*, Niles, IL: Argus Communications, 1977, pp. 6, 7).

Excerpts from the Tao Te King: Principles of Taoism

The following excerpts from The *Tao Te King* demonstrate the basic thought of Taoism (translation by James Legge):

Chapter I: The Tao That Can Be Trodden

The Tao that can be trodden is not the enduring and unchanging Tao. The name that can be named is not the enduring and unchanging name.

Conceived of as having no name, it is the Originator of heaven and earth; conceived of as having a name, it is the Mother of all things.

> Always without desire we must be found,
> If its deep mystery we would sound;
> But if desire always within us be,
> Its outer fringe is all that we shall see.

Under these two aspects, it is really the same; but as development takes place, it receives the different names. Together we call them the Mystery. Where the Mystery is the deepest is the gate of all that is subtle and wonderful.

Chapter LVI: He Who Knows the Tao

He who knows the Tao does not care to speak about it; he who is ever ready to speak about it does not know it.

He who knows it will keep his mouth shut and close the portals of his nostrils. He will blunt his sharp points and unravel the complications of things; he will temper his brightness, and bring himself into agreement with the obscurity of others. This is called "the Mysterious Agreement."

Such a one cannot be treated familiarly or distantly; he is beyond all consideration of profit or injury; of nobility or meanness—he is the noblest man under heaven.

Chapter LXIII: It Is the Way

It is the way of the Tao to act without thinking of acting;
To conduct affairs without feeling the trouble of them;
To taste without discerning any flavor;
To consider what is small as great, and a few as many; and
To recompense injury with kindness.

The master of it anticipates things that are difficult while they are easy, and does things that would become great while they are small.

All difficult things in the world are sure to arise from a previous state in which they were easy, and all great things from one in which they were small. Therefore the sage, while he never does what is great, is able on that account to accomplish the greatest things.

He who lightly promises is sure to keep but little faith; he who is continually thinking things easy is sure to find them difficult. Therefore the sage sees difficulty even in what seems easy, and so never has any difficulties.

Chapter XXV: There Was Something

There was something undefined and complete, coming into existence before Heaven and Earth. How still it was and formless, standing alone, and undergoing no change, reaching everywhere and in no danger of being exhausted! It may be regarded as the Mother of all things.

I do not know its name, and I give it the designation of the Tao (the Way or Course). Making an effort further to give it a name I call it The Great.

Great, it passes on in constant flow. Passing on, it becomes remote. Having become remote, it returns. Therefore the Tao is great; Heaven is great; Earth is great; and the sage king is also great. In the universe there are four that are great, and the sage king is one of them.

Man takes his law from the Earth; the Earth takes its law from Heaven; Heaven takes its law from the Tao. The law of the Tao is its being what it is.

So, in their beautiful array,
Things form and never know decay.

How know I that it is so with all the beauties of existing things? By this nature of the Tao.

Chapter LI: All Things

All things are produced by the Tao, and nourished by its outflowing operation.

They receive their forms according to the nature of each, and are completed according to the circumstances of their condition.

Therefore all things without exception honor the Tao, and exalt its outflowing operation.

This honoring of the Tao and exalting of its operation are not the result of any ordination, but always a spontaneous tribute.

Thus it is that the Tao produces all things, nourishes them, brings them to their full growth, nurses them, completes them, matures them, maintains them, and overspreads them.

It produces them and makes no claim to the possession of them;

It carries them through their processes and does not vaunt its ability in doing so;

It brings them to maturity and exercises no control over them;

This is called its mysterious operation.

The Way is like an empty vessel which is the ancestry from which come all things in the world.

The value of an act is judged by its timing.

Thirty spokes unite in the hub, but the worth of the wheel will depend on the void where the axle turns.

What gives a clay cup value is the empty space its walls create.

Usefulness is to be found in non-existence.

If you know righteousness, though you die, you shall not perish.

If you trust people not enough, they may trust you not at all.

Get rid of your preachers and discard your teachers, and the people will benefit a hundredfold. Root out your schemers and renounce your profiteers, and thieving will disappear.

Between "yes" and "no" how small the difference; between "good" and "evil" how great the difference.

He who is not a competitor, no one in the whole world can compete with him.

If you work by the Way, you will be of the Way.

Little faith is put in those who have little faith.

There is something that existed before the earth and the sky began and its name is the Way.

Man conforms to the earth; the earth conforms to the sky; the sky conforms to the Way; the Way conforms to its own nature.

As for those who would take the whole world to tinker with as they see fit, observe that they never succeed.

The wise reject all extremes.

Those who are on the Way might be compared to rivulets flowing into the sea.

He who understands others is wise; he who understands himself is enlightened.

He who conquers others is strong; he who conquers his own will is mighty.

If you would take, you must first give, this is the beginning of intelligence.

Absence of desires brings tranquility.

A cart is more than the sum of its parts.

The Way is nameless and hidden, yet all things gain their fulfillment in it.

To the good I would be good, and to the bad I would be good; in that way all might become good.

Wars are best waged by stratagem; but people are best governed by forthrightness.

The more prohibitions, the more poverty; the more laws, the more crimes; the more skills, the more luxuries; the more weapons, the more chaos.

In serving Heaven and in ruling men use moderation.

Everything difficult must be dealt with while it is still easy.

A thousand-mile journey can be made one step at a time.

Three things prize above all: gentleness, frugality and humility. For the gentle can be bold, the frugal can be liberal and the humble can become leaders of men.

If you cannot advance an inch, retreat a foot.

Philosophical and Religious Taoism
Philosophical

Taoism has historically taken two different roads. Taoism as a philosophy, or philosophical Taoism, began around 300 B.C. Emphasizing the Tao as the source of ultimate reality, philosophical Taoism attempted to put man in touch with the harmony of nature by allowing him to exercise freely his instincts and imaginations.

Religious Taoism began forming around the second century A.D. when the emperor Huan ordered a temple built in honor of Lao-tzu, with offerings also being made to him. However, as a formal religion Taoism did not actually make an appearance until the seventh century. John B. Noss explains why this occurred:

> By this time Buddhism had made its appearance as a great and significant factor in Chinese religious life. Neither Confucianism, the rather stiff and formal mode of thought

and behavior known chiefly to the literati and officials, nor Taoism, still the preoccupation either of intellectuals on the one hand or of students of the esoteric and the occult on the other, was wholly satisfactory to the unlearned and lowly masses. Hinayana Buddhism was no better in the eyes of these unlettered but spiritually hungry souls, but the Mahayana was another matter. The beneficent Bodhisattvas who gave aid in daily life and the Dhyani Buddhas who admitted one to paradise, were soon being plied with gifts and prayers by millions.

As Buddhism swept across China and into Korea, the Taoists, struck with amazement and yet sure that China had her own resources, so to speak, in the way of gods and spirits, began to look into their own heritage, and finding much to value, they began to ape the powerful faith brought in from India (John B. Noss, *Man's Religions*, New York: MacMillan Company, 1969, p. 272).

Religious

Religious Taoism had sacred scripture, a priesthood, temples and disciples. There was also an eschatological belief that a new age would come about, overthrowing the old established order. As time went on, gods were brought into the religious system along with belief in heaven and hell and eventually the deification of Lao-tzu.

Noss reports on the present state of Taoism:

Taoism has for many years been in decline. According to the latest reports, as a religion it is now dead. The government frowns upon it and is determined to suppress it. But many still cling to it as magic, no matter how secret they must be about it nor how carefully they must try to elude the vigilant eye of the Communist district leaders (*Ibid.*, p. 274).

Taoism and Christianity

In his book *The World's Living Religions*, Robert E. Hume lists the following weaknesses in Taoism:

Its not sufficiently personal and responsible Supreme Being.

Its founder's positively ignoble example of withdrawing from difficulty; not organizing for reform.

Its inadequate recognition of the evils in the world.

Its inadequate appreciation of physical facts and resources, discouraging to scientific inquiry.

Its over-emphasis on inactivity *(Wu-Wei)*, belittling to human effort.

Its lack of a commanding enthusiastic principle for living; mostly negative advice.

Its ethical ideal of indifference and irresponsibility.

Its inadequate conception of immortal life; merely a protracted existence.

Its lack of a program for the uplift of society; only a return to an uncivilized simplicity.

Its relapse into polytheism, demonolatry, and practice of magic (Hume, *op. cit.*, p. 151).

Although Taoism may have run its course in China, it is a very real threat in the West. With the hippie generation the United States saw the advent of the "tune out, drop out" mentality, a mentality completely suited to Taoist philosophy.

We can rest assured, however, that even though the Tao may have a temporary appeal, it ultimately cannot fulfill its disciples. The impersonal Tao is in stark contrast to the personal loving God of Christianity, who is both willing and able to meet the deepest needs we all have.

The Bible says, "Come to Me, all who are weary and heavy laden, and I will give you rest. Take My yoke upon you, and learn from Me, for I am gentle and humble in heart; and you shall find rest for your souls. For My yoke is easy, and My load is light" (Matthew 11:28-30 NASB).

Taoism has no real answer to the problem of evil, for the Taoist "solution" of ignoring or withdrawing from the ills of society does nothing to cure those very real ills.

Jesus, on the other hand, taught His disciples to get involved with the problems of the world. "Go therefore and make disciples of all the nations, baptizing them in the name of the Father and the Son and the Holy Spirit" (Matthew 28:19 NASB). "But you shall receive power when the Holy Spirit has come upon you; and you shall be My witnesses both in Jerusalem, and in all Judea and Sumaria, and even to the remotest part of the earth" (Acts 1:8 NASB).

God, through Jesus Christ, got involved with the problems we all face and provided a once-and-for-all solution by His death on the cross. The near extinction of the religious side of Taoism is a testimony to the fact that it doesn't meet our deepest needs. God in Jesus Christ made the ultimate identification with our suffering and by it, secured our salvation from it.

"Since then the children share in flesh and blood, He Himself likewise also partook of the same, that through death He might render powerless him who had the power of death, that is, the devil; and might deliver those who through fear of death were subject to slavery all their lives... Therefore, He had to be made like His brethren in all things, that He might become a merciful and faithful high priest in things pertaining to God, to make propitiation for the sins of the people. For since He Himself was tempted in that which He has suffered, He is able to come to the aid of those who are tempted" (Hebrews 2:14, 15, 17, 18 NASB).

Taoistic Terms

CHUANG TZU—A later disciple of Lao-Tzu who wrote some 33 books which helped popularize Taoism.

LAO-TZU—Chinese sage and philosopher who founded Taoism.

TAO TE KING—Literally translated, "The Way and Its Power." This small book, supposedly written by Lao-Tzu, is the sacred scripture of Taoism. The work advocates enduring the hardships of the world through non-involvement, thereby giving the individual a better chance for survival. Sometimes called *Lao-Tzu*, after its supposed author.

THE TAO—Literally, the "Way" or "Path." The Tao is the inexpressible way of ultimate reality by which one should order his life.

WU WEI—The concept of inaction, taught in the *Tao Te King.* By practicing *Wu Wei*, one can get his life in harmony with the Tao and live as he is meant to live.

YIN-YANG—The Yin and Yang represent elements in the universe that are contrary to each other, such as life and death, light and darkness, good and evil. The Yang represents positive elements, the Yin the negative elements.

Taoism Bibliography

Bush, Richard C., *The Story of Religion in China*, Niles, IL: Argus Communications, 1977.

Chan, Wing-Tsit, ed., *A Sourcebook in Chinese Philosophy*, Princeton, NJ: Princeton University Press, 1963.

Hume, Robert E., *The World's Living Religions*, New York: Charles Scribner's Sons, rev. ed., 1959.

Mueller, Max, ed., *Sacred Books of the East*, London: Krishna Press, 1879-1910.

Noss, John B., *Man's Religions*, New York: MacMillan Company, 1969.

Rawlings, Maurice, *Life-Wish: Reincarnation: Reality or Hoax*, Nashville: Thomas Nelson Inc., 1981.

Shintoism

Shinto, the national religion of Japan, is one of the oldest of all the world's religions. It is unlike other religions inasmuch as it is basically not a system of beliefs. It has been variously defined. John B. Noss' definition states:

> It is basically a reverent loyalty to familiar ways of life and familiar places... it is true to say that for the masses in Japan love of country, as in other lands, is a matter of the heart first, and of doctrinal substance second (John B. Noss, *Man's Religions*, New York: MacMillan Company, 1969, p. 316).

Clark B. Offner defines Shinto in the following manner:

> Shinto denotes "the traditional religious practices which originated in Japan and developed mainly among the Japanese people along with the underlying life attitudes and ideology which support such practices." Various implications can immediately be derived from this statement of a modern Shinto scholar. First, Shinto does not refer to an organized, clearly-defined body of doctrine nor to a unified, systematized code of behaviour. The origins of Shinto are lost in the hazy mists enshrouding the ancient period of Japanese history, but from the time the Japanese people became conscious of their own cultural character and traditions, the practices, attitudes and ideology that eventually developed into the Shinto of today were already included within them (Clark B. Offner, in *The World's Religions*, Sir Norman Anderson, ed., Grand Rapids: William B. Eerdmans Publishing Company, 1976, p. 190).

Shinto History

Shinto is purely a Japanese religion, the origins of which are buried in antiquity. The Japanese are a people who love their land and believe the islands of Japan were the first divine creation. This idea of the divine origin of their land is very old and goes hand-in-hand with the beliefs of Shinto. This national idealism, the love of their country, is basically why Shinto has been limited to Japan. John B. Noss comments:

> The Japanese came early to the belief that their land was divine, but late to the nationalistic dogma that no other land is divine, that the divinity of Japan is so special and unique, so absent elsewhere, as to make Japan "center of this phenomenal world" (John B. Noss, *op. cit.*, p. 316).

The Japanese name for their country is *Nippon*, which means "sun origin." Until the end of World War II, Japanese children were taught at school that the emperors were descendants of the sun-goddess, *Amaterasu*. *Amaterasu* had allegedly given the imperial house the divine right to rule. In 1946, in a radio broadcast to the Japanese people, Emperor Hirohito repudiated his divine right to rule.

Early Development

Shinto's history can be divided into a number of stages. The first period was from prehistoric times to 552 A.D. when Shinto reigned supreme among the people of Japan without any serious competition.

In 552 A.D. Buddhism started gaining in popularity among the Japanese people. In the year 645 A.D., the Emperor Kotoku embraced Buddhism and rejected Shinto.

From A.D. 800 to 1700, Shinto became combined with other religions, mixing with both Buddhism and Confucianism and forming what is called *Ryobu Shinto*, or dual-aspect Shinto. Shinto, by itself, experienced a considerable decline during this period.

Revival

Around 1700 Shinto experienced a revival when the study of archaic Japanese texts was reinstituted. One of the most learned Shinto scholars of the period was Hirata, who wrote:

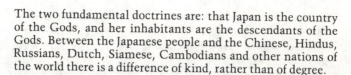

The two fundamental doctrines are: that Japan is the country of the Gods, and her inhabitants are the descendants of the Gods. Between the Japanese people and the Chinese, Hindus, Russians, Dutch, Siamese, Cambodians and other nations of the world there is a difference of kind, rather than of degree.

The Mikado is the true Son of Heaven, who is entitled to reign over the four seas and the ten-thousand countries.

From the fact of the divine descent of the Japanese people proceeds their immeasurable superiority to the natives of other countries in courage and intelligence. They "are honest and upright of heart, and are not given to useless theorizing and falsehoods like other nations" (Cited by Robert E. Hume, *The World's Living Religions*, New York: Charles Scribner's Sons, rev. ed., 1959, p. 172).

These ideas revitalized Shinto among the Japanese people since it re-established the divine origin of the land and the people of Japan.

State Religion

Japanese Emperor Meiji established Shinto as the official religion of Japan in place of Buddhism. However, since the people continued to embrace both religions, in 1877 Buddhism was allowed to be practiced by the people, with total religious liberty granted two years afterward.

State Shinto, which is to be regarded as a patriotic ritual by the citizens irrespective of their religion, paid homage to the Emperor, and was established in 1882. This soon became, for all intents and purposes, the state religion. After the military victories of Japan in World War I, the idea of the divinity of the Emperor became solidly entrenched again in the people. It was not until the defeat of World War II that state Shinto was abolished as the religion of the Japanese people. With the fall of state Shinto, the shrines no longer came under government control and are now supported by private means.

Meaning of Shinto

The word Shinto comes from the Chinese word *Shen-tao*, which means "the way of the gods." This term was not applied to the religion until the sixth century A.D., in order to distinguish it from Buddhism. A major feature of Shinto is the notion of *kami*. *Kami* is a difficult term to define precisely but it refers basically to the concept of sacred power in both animate and inanimate objects. Ninian Smart elaborates upon the idea of *kami* in the following manner:

> Shintoism displayed, and still displays, a powerful sense of the presence of gods and spirits in nature. These spirits are called *kami*, literally "superior beings," and it is appropriate to venerate them. The kami are too numerous to lend themselves to a systematic ordering or stable hierarchy, but among the many the sun goddess Amaterasu has long held a central place in Shinto belief. According to the myth found at the beginning of the *Kojiki*, the earliest of the celestial gods who came into being instructed Izanagi and Izanami, male and female deities of the second generation of gods, to create the world, and in particular the islands of Japan (the two were in effect identified).
>
> Through the process of sexual generation they produced the land, and the kami of the mountains, trees, and streams, the god of the wind and the god of fire, and so on. Eventually...the goddess Amaterasu, the great kami of the Sun, came into being. Possibly, prior to the mythological account of her origin she was the mother goddess of the Yamato clans; the mythology may reflect the way in which the other deities were successively replaced in the earliest period, and then were put under the dominance of the chief kami of the Yamato. But the line between kami and human is not a sharp one, however exalted some of the deities may be.
>
> The Japanese people themselves, according to the traditional myths, are descended from the kami; while the line of emperors traces its descent back to Amaterasu. Amaterasu sent her son Ni-ni-gi down to rule Japan for her, and thence the imperial line took its origin (this tradition in recent times was given exaggerated emphasis in order to make Shinto into an ideology justifying a nationalistic expansionist policy). The line, too, between the personal and impersonal in the kami is fluid. Some of the spirits associated with particular places or things are not strongly personalized, though the mythology concerned with the great gods and goddesses is fully anthropomorphic (Ninian Smart, *The Religious Experience of Mankind*, New York: Charles Scribner's Sons, 1969, pp. 192, 193).

Sacred Books

Although Shinto does not consider any one volume as the wholly inspired revelation on which its religion is based, two books are considered sacred and have done much to influence the beliefs of the Japanese people. These works are *Ko-ji-ki*, the "records of ancient matters," and *Nihon-gi*, the "chronicles of Japan." They were both composed around 720 A.D. and in that they report events occurring some 1300 years earlier in the history of Japan, they are to be considered late works.

The *Ko-ji-ki* is the oldest existing written record in Japanese. The work contains myth, legend and historical narrative in relating the story of Japan, the imperial ancestors and the imperial court. The work was compiled around 712 A.D.

The *Nihon-gi*, compiled around 720 A.D., chronicles the origin of Japan up until 700 A.D.

Types of Shinto

Since Shinto has neither a founder, sacred writings, nor any authoritative set of beliefs, there are great diversities in the two types of Shinto practiced and the beliefs held. Some Shinto groups do claim a founder, authoritative scriptures, and specific doctrine. These groups are designated sects of Shinto. However, the majority of practitioners have no such set beliefs but worship freely at various shrines located throughout Japan. This practice of *Shrine Shinto* is usually identified with the term *Shinto*.

Worship

The basic place for worship in Shinto is at one of the numerous shrines covering the country of Japan. Although many Shintoists have built altars in their homes, the center of worship is the local shrine. Since Shinto has a large number of deities, a systematic worship of all such deities is impossible. The Shinto religious books acknowledge that only a few deities are consistently worshipped, the chief being the sun-goddess, *Amaterasu*.

There is a grand imperial shrine dedicated to the worship of *Amaterasu* at Ise, some 200 miles southwest of Tokyo. This centralized place of worship is the most sacred spot in all of Japan. The practice of worshipping at this particular spot has its roots before the time of Christ.

It is here that the Shintoists make a pilgrimage to worship at the outer court, while the inner court is reserved for the priests and government officials.

Amaterasu is the chief deity of Shinto and is feminine rather than masculine. That the highest object of worship from whom the divine ancestors arose is a female rather than a male deity is unique among the larger world religions.

A Shinto Prayer

The following Shinto prayer, found in the *Yengishiki*, shows the Shintoists' intermingling of their spiritual feeling with nature:

> I declare in the great presence of the From-Heaven-shining-great-deity who sits in Ise.
>
> Because the Sovereign great goddess bestows on him the countries of the four quarters over which her glance extends,
>
> As far as the limit where Heaven stands up like a wall,
> As far as the bounds where the country stands up distant,
> As far as the limit where the blue clouds spread flat,
> As far as the bounds where the white clouds lie away fallen —
>
> The blue sea plain as far as the limit whither come the prows of the ships without drying poles or paddles,
> The ships which continuously crowd on the great sea plain,
> And the roads which men travel by land, as far as the limit whither come the horses' hoofs, with the baggage-cords tied tightly, treading the uneven rocks and tree-roots and standing up continuously in a long path without a break —
>
> Making the narrow countries wide and the hilly countries plain,
> And as it were drawing together the distant countries by throwing many tens of ropes over them —
>
> He will pile up the first-fruits like a range of hills in the great presence of the Sovereign great goddess, and will peacefully enjoy the remainder.

Shinto and Christianity

The religion of Shinto is in opposition to Christianity. The fact that Shinto in its purest form teaches the superiority of the Japanese people and their land above all others on earth is diametrically opposed to the teaching of the Bible. According to the Bible, the Jews are God's chosen people through whom He entrusted His words.

"Then what advantage has the Jew? or what is the benefit of circumcision? Great in every respect. First of all, that they were entrusted with the oracles of God" (Romans 3:1, 2, NASB). However, though the Jews are God's chosen people, they have never been designated better than any other people (Galatians 3:27) and they have never been taught that they were direct descendants of the gods, as Shinto teaches.

Shintoism fosters a pride and a feeling of superiority in the Japanese people. This type of pride is condemned by God, who says, "There is none righteous, not even one" (Romans 3:10, NASB). The same lesson was learned by the Apostle Peter who concluded: "I most certainly understand now that God is not one to show partiality, but in every nation the man who fears Him and does what is right, is welcome to Him" (Acts 10:34, NASB).

Since Shinto teaches the basic goodness and divine origin of its people, there is no need for a Savior. This is the natural consequence of assuming one's race is of celestial origin.

Christianity teaches that all of us need a savior because our sins need to be punished. God, through Jesus Christ, took that punishment on Himself so that all mankind could be brought back into a proper relationship with Him. "Namely, that God was in Christ reconciling the world to Himself, not counting their trespasses against them, and He has committed to us the word of reconciliation. Therefore, we are ambassadors for Christ, as though God were entreating through us; we beg you on behalf of Christ, be reconciled to God. He made Him who knew no sin to be sin on our behalf, that we might become the righteousness of God in Him" (2 Corinthians 5:19-21, NASB).

Furthermore, the *Ko-ji-ki* and *Nihon-gi*, as the basis of the Shinto myth, are found to be hopelessly unhistorical and totally unverifiable. The stories and legends contained in these works are a far cry from the historically verifiable documents of both the Old and New Testaments.

The concept of *kami* is both polytheistic and crude, surrounded by much superstition. This is in contrast to the God of the Bible whose ways are righteous and beyond reproach. Immorality abounds in the stories of Shinto while the Bible is quick to condemn acts of immorality.

> The Bible deals very frankly with the sins of its characters. Read the biographies today, and see how they try to cover up, overlook or ignore the shady side of people. Take the great literary geniuses; most are painted as saints. The Bible does not do it that way. It simply tells it like it is:
>
> The sins of the people denounced—Deuteronomy 9:24
>
> Sins of the patriarchs—Genesis 12:11-13; 49:5-7
>
> Evangelists paint their own faults and the faults of the apostles—Matthew 8:10-26; 26:31-56; Mark 6:52; 8:18; Luke 8:24, 25; 9:40-45; John 10:6; 16:32
>
> Disorder of the churches—1 Corinthians 1:11; 15:12; 2 Corinthians 2:4, etc.
>
> (Josh McDowell, *Evidence That Demands a Verdict*, San Bernardino, CA: Campus Crusade for Christ International, 1972, p. 23).

Shinto finds little acceptance apart from Japan since everything of Japanese origin is exalted and that which is non-Japanese is abased. Shinto is a textbook example of a religion invented by man to explain his ancestry and environment while taking no consideration of anyone but himself.

Shintoistic Terms

AMATERASU—The sun-goddess, the chief deity worshipped in Shintoism.

BUSHIDO CODE—Literally, "the warrior-knight-way." The code practiced by the military class of the feudal period (Samurai) which has held a fascination with the Japanese people throughout its history. The code is an unwritten system of behavior stressing loyalty to emperor and country.

EMPEROR MEIJI—The Japanese emperor who established Shinto as the state religion of Japan.

HARAKIRI—The ceremonial suicide committed by the Bushido warrior performed as an atonement for failure or bad judgment. The warrior believed death was to be preferred to disgrace.

HONDON—The inner sanctuary of a Shinto shrine in which is housed the Shintai, or "god body."

IZANAGI—The "female-who-invites." The female deity who, according to the Shinto myth, gave birth to the eight islands of Japan.

IZANAMI—The "male-who-invites." The male deity who, along with the female deity Izanagi, helped produce the Japanese islands and the Japanese people.

JIGAI—The method of suicide consisting of cutting the jugular vein. It is committed by females as an atonement for their sins.

KAMI—The sacred power found in both animate and inanimate objects. This power is deified in Shintoism.

KAMI DAMA—"The god shelf" which is found in most private homes on which are placed memorial tablets with the names of an ancestor or deity inscribed on it.

KO-JI-KI—The "records of ancient matters" composed in 712 A.D., charting the imperial ancestors and the imperial court.

MIKADO—A term used by foreigners to designate the emperor of Japan.

NIHON-GI—The "chronicles of Japan" composed around 720 A.D. This work is a history of Japan from its origin until 700 A.D.

O-HARAI—"The Great Purification." The greatest of all Shinto ceremonies by which the people go through a national purging of their sins.

RYOBU SHINTO—Also known as, "dual aspect Shinto." The term refers to the mixing of Shintoism with Buddhism and Confucianism.

SHINTAI—An object of worship housed in the inner sanctuary of a Shinto shrine. The Shintai is usually an object of little value, such as a sword or mirror, but it supposedly contains magical powers and consequently is viewed as a good-luck charm.

SHINTO—The term *Shinto* is derived from the Chinese term, *Shen-tao*, meaning the "way of the higher spirits." *Shinto* is the designation for the religion that has long characterized Japan and its people.

SHINTO MYTH — The belief that the islands of Japan and the Japanese people are of divine origin.

STATE SHINTO — The patriotic ritual, established in 1882, which worshipped the emperor as the direct descendant of the gods. State Shinto was abolished at the end of World War II.

Shintoism Bibliography

Hume, Robert E., *The World's Living Religions*, New York: Charles Scribner's Sons, rev. ed., 1959.

Noss, John B., *Man's Religions*, New York: MacMillan Company, 1974.

Offner, Clark B. in *The World's Religions*, Sir Norman Anderson, ed., Grand Rapids, MI: William B. Eerdmans Publishing Company, 1976.

Smart, Ninian, *The Religious Experience of Mankind*, New York: Charles Scribner's Sons, 1969.

Zoroastrianism

Zoroastrianism, a unique religion which stresses the eternal battle of good versus evil, has had a larger impact than its small number of followers (100,000) would suggest. It is the religion of one man who lived some 600 years before the birth of Christ. His name was Zoroaster. The religiously fertile area of Babylonia (modern Iraq and Iran) was his home.

History

Zoroaster

The founder of Zoroastrianism was the man Zoroaster (a Greek corruption of the old Iranian word *Zarathushtra*). His time and place of birth are unknown, but it is generally believed that he was born around 650 B.C. in Persia (present-day Iran). However, as Richard Cavendish observed, there is much doubt as to when and where Zoroaster was born:

> The early history of Zoroastrianism is much in dispute. The religion was founded by Zoroaster (the Greek form of his name, which is Zarathushtra in Persian), but it is not certain when he lived, where he lived or how much of later Zoroastrianism came from him. Tradition puts him in western Iran in the sixth century B.C., a little earlier than the Buddha in India, but it is now thought that he lived in northeastern Iran, in the area on the borders of modern Afghanistan

and Turkmenistan. An alternative theory dates him much earlier, somewhere in the period from 1700 to 1500 B.C., and places him in the plains of Central Asia, perhaps before the first groups of Aryans moved south from the plains into Iran and India (Richard Cavendish, *The Great Religions*, New York: Arco Publishing Company, 1980, p. 125).

Tradition says that Zoroaster was the son of a camel merchant and grew up at a time when his fellow Persians worshipped many gods. While growing up he had a keen interest in religion, pondering the mysteries of life. At an early age he became known for his compassionate nature, especially toward the elderly.

Zoroaster had an excellent education, studying with some of the best teachers in Persia. Yet he became restless, and at age 20 he left his father and mother in a search for answers to life's deepest questions. He would seek, from all those whom he met, answers to his religious questions.

During this time of Zoroaster's religious quest, it is said he used his medical ability to help heal those ravaged by the ongoing wars. It was at age 30 that Zoroaster received enlightenment. As the account goes, Zoroaster received a vision on the banks of the Daitya River when a large figure appeared to him. This personage identified himself as *Vohu Manah*, or "good thought." This figure took Zoroaster into the presence of the wise lord *Ahura Mazda*, who instructed Zoroaster in the true religion.

Zoroaster spent the next ten years proclaiming his newly discovered truth but had little success. The movement began to grow after Zoroaster converted a prince named Vishtaspa, who helped propagate his new-found faith. During the ensuing years the faith spread rapidly. Zoroastrian tradition records two holy wars which were fought over the faith, the second of which took the life of Zoroaster at age 77. However, though the prophet died, the faith remained alive. Zoroastrianism quickly destroyed the magic and idol worship prevalent then and established its own belief in one god, a heaven, and a hell (see Maurice Rawlings, *Life-Wish: Reincarnation: Reality or Hoax*, Nashville: Thomas Nelson Inc., 1981, p. 63).

The Deification of Zoroaster

As is true with many religious leaders, the later disciples of Zoroaster, far removed in time from their master, made him an object of veneration. Thus, Zoroaster became an object of worship along with the deity *Ahura-Mazda*. He is lauded in the following terms:

> Head of the two-footed race; the wisest of all beings in the perfection of his holiness; the only one who can daunt evil (Max Mueller, ed., *Secret Books of the East*, Oxford: Krishna Press, 1897-1910, 23:190, 229, 275).

> The chieftainship of all things was from Zoroaster; the completely good, the righteous Zoroaster (*Ibid.*, 5:88; 18:90).

> Incomparable among mankind through his desire for righteousness, and his understanding the means of defeating the destroyer, and teaching creatures (*Ibid.*, 37:241).

> A heavenly radiance "came down from the endless light" to the grandmother of Zoroaster for his birth from a radiantly wonderful virgin mother (*Ibid.*, 47:18-20, 138-139).

> He was pre-existent, 3,000 years before his physical birth, and during the interval he remained with the archangels equal to the archangels (*Ibid.*, 47:21, 22, 122).

Present-day Status

Richard Cavendish sums up the present-day status of Zoroastrianism:

> The principal religions of the world count their adherents in the millions, and on this scale it almost needs a microscope to see Zoroastrianism at all. There are about 100,000 Zoroastrians in India and Pakistan, where they are called Parsis. They do not accept converts and their numbers are steadily diminishing. There are also a few thousand Zoroastrians in Iran, and smaller communities in North America, Britain, East Africa and Hong Kong. Despite its comparative poverty in numbers, however, Zoroastrianism is enormously rich in ideas, which have had an influence far beyond its own ranks (Richard Cavendish, *op. cit.*, p. 125).

Because of the influence it exerts, Zoroastrianism is still a religion to be reckoned with.

The Avesta

The sacred scripture of the Zoroastrians is known as the *Avesta*, originally written in an old Iranian language called

Avestan. Of the original work only a small fraction has survived, with the total size about one-tenth that of the Bible. The *Avesta* contains hymns, prayers and ritual instruction. It is divided into three major sections, the oldest of which is called *Yasna*.

Within the *Yasna* there is a group of five hymns known as the *Gathas*, which are composed in a more archaic dialect than the remainder of the *Avesta*. These hymns are generally assumed to be the closest account we have of the very words of Zoroaster.

The *Gathas* stress the lordship of *Ahura-Mazda* as the only supreme God, along with an exhortation to righteous living. The *Gathas* also reveal that the righteous will receive a reward at the end of this present age.

The second major section is called the *Yashts* and contains hymns to various deities. The third section is known as the *Vidēvdāt* (or *Vendīdād*) and is a section written much later, containing the law against the demons along with other codes and regulations.

The priests of Zoroastrianism are called *magi* and use magic in their communion with God. This is the source for our English word "magic."

Ahura-Mazda

According to Zoroaster, there is one true deity to be worshipped. His name is *Ahura-Mazda* (wise lord). The opening lines of the *Avesta* exalt this deity:

> Ahura-Mazda, the creator, radiant, glorious, greatest and best, most beautiful, most firm, wisest, most perfect, the most bounteous spirit! (Max Mueller, ed., *op. cit.*, 31:195-196).

The *Gathas* attribute the following characteristics to *Ahura-Mazda*:

Creator: (*Yasna*, 31:7, 11; 44:7; 50:11; 51:7.)
All-seeing: (*Yasna*, 31:13; 44:2.)
All-knowing: (*Yasna*, 31:13; 45:3; 48:2-3.)
Most mighty, greatest:(*Yasna*, 28:5; 33:11; 45:6.)
Friendly: (*Yasna*, 31:21; 44:2; 4:2.)
Father of Justice or Right, *Asha:* (*Yasna*, 44:3; 47:2.)
Father of Good Mind, *Vohu Manah:* (*Yasna*, 31:8; 45:4.)

Beneficent, *hudae*: (*Yasna*, 45:6; 48:3.)

Bountiful, *spenta*: (*Yasna*, 43:4, 5, 7, 9, 11, 13, 15; 44:2; 45:5; 46:9; 48:3; 51:10.)

Most bountiful spirit, *spenishta mainyu*: (*Yasna*, 30:5.)

Angra Mainyu

Although *Ahura-Mazda* is the supreme deity, he is opposed by another powerful force known as *Angra Mainyu*, or *Ahriman*, "the bad spirit." From the beginning of existence these two antagonistic spirits have been at odds with each other:

> Now the two primal Spirits, who revealed themselves in vision as Twins, are the Better and the Bad in thought and word and action. And between these two the wise once chose aright, the foolish not so. And when these twain Spirits came together in the beginning, they established Life and Not-Life, and that at the last the Worst Existence (Hell) shall be to the followers of the Lie, but the Best Thought (Paradise) to him that follows Right. Of these twain Spirits he that followed the Lie *chose* doing the worst things; the holiest Spirit *chose* Right (James Hope Moulton, *Early Zoroastrianism*, London: Constable and Company, 1913, *Yasna* 30:3-5, p. 349).

These two powers have been co-equal from the beginning of time and will continue to battle each other until the end of the world. As Zoroastrian doctrine developed, both *Ahura-Mazda* and *Angra Mainyu* were given seven attributes (known as the *Amesha-stentas*) which were corresponding opposites:

Ahura-Mazda	Angra Mainyu
Ahura-Mazda (God of light, wisdom)	*Angra Mainyu* (Prince of darkness)
Asha (right, justice)	*Druj* (falsehood)
Vohu monah (good mind)	*Akem* (evil mind)
Kshathra (power)	*Dush-kshathra* (cowardice)
Armaiti (love)	*Taromaiti* (false pretense)
Haurvatat (health)	*Avetat* (misery)
Ameretat (immortality)	*Merethyn* (annihilation)

Future Judgment

Zoroastrianism was one of the earliest religions to teach

an ultimate triumph of good over evil. There would be punishment in the end for the wicked and reward for the righteous. The following portions of the *Gathas* present this doctrine:

Yasna 30:2, 4, 9-11; 31:8, 19; 32:6, 15; 33:3, 5; 43:12; 45:7; 46:12; 48:4; 51:6; 53:7-9

Influence Upon Other Religions

One of the claims made by some religious scholars is that Zoroastrianism has had a profound effect in shaping the doctrines of three major religions: Judaism, Islam and Christianity. Consider the following assertions:

The importance of Zoroastrianism has always been qualitative rather than quantitative. Its highest significance lies in the influence it has exercised on the development of at least three other great religions. First, it made contributions to Judaism, for between 538 B.C. (when the Persians under Cyrus captured Babylonia and set free the Jews exiled in that land) and 330 B.C. (when the Persian Empire was destroyed by Alexander) the Jews were directly under the suzerainty of the Zoroastrians. And it was from the suzerains that the Jews first learnt to believe in an Ahriman, a personal devil, whom they called in Hebrew, Satan. Possibly from them, too, the Jews first learnt to believe in a heaven and hell, and in a Judgment Day for each individual (Lewis Browne, *This Believing World*, New York: MacMillan Company, 1926, pp. 216, 217).

Influence on the Bible

Of all the other nine extra-Biblical living religions, Zoroastrianism is the only one from which a definite religious belief has been borrowed and included in the Bible. Consistently throughout the Old Testament down to and including the Isaiah of the Exile, the ultimate source of everything, including evil, is represented as the God Jehovah. But a distinct change took place after the Exile. A comparison of two parallel accounts of a certain experience of King David will show that a post-exilic document (1 Chronicles 21:1) substitutes "Satan" for "Jehovah" in the pre-exilic account (2 Samuel 24:1). Thus Satan is not an original feature of the Bible, but was introduced from Zoroastrianism.

Perhaps certain other innovations besides the idea of a Satan were adopted from Zoroastrianism by the Hebrews after they had come into direct contact with that religion in the Babylonian Exile: for example, the ideas of an elaborate angelology and demonology, of a great Saviour or Deliverer to come, of a final resurrection and divine Judgment, and a definitely picturable future life. Certainly Jesus' word "Paradise" (Greek, *paradeisos*, Luke 23:43) was, at least etymologically, derived form Persian origin (Avestan, *pairidaeza*)(Robert E. Hume, *The World's Living Religions*, New York: Charles Scribner's Sons, rev. ed., 1959, p. 200).

Although many teach that Zoroastrianism has had a profound influence upon the teachings of the Bible, we believe this is not the case at all.

In other works *(Answers, Reasons)* we have demonstrated that Christianity is not a man-made religion, as many assume, but it is rather the one true faith supernaturally revealed by the true and living God. The Bible claims to be God's unique revelation of Himself, and we have shown the evidence that leads one in that direction. If this be true, then the practices of other religions, including Zoroastrianism, could not have affected Biblical doctrine as is claimed.

Those who claim Zoroastrianism has had an effect on the Bible begin with the inherent assumption that the Old Testament was written later than the traditional evidence shows. Many books, such as the Pentateuch (Genesis-Deuteronomy), Job and Isaiah chapters 40-66, are wrongly dated during or after the exile (ca 536 B.C.) instead of as early as 1300 B.C. Consequently, when these concepts appear in certain biblical books, they are given a late date because they are already assumed to have been influenced by other religions.

In *More Evidence That Demands a Verdict* (written by Josh McDowell), we see that these assumptions of the late dating of the Old Testament are anything but assured. If one accepts the traditional dating of the Old Testament, then the proverbial shoe is on the other foot. It is not Zoroastrianism that influenced biblical doctrine when the Jews were in exile under Persian rule; it is the Bible that influenced Zoroastrianism!

Moreover, the ideas that are suposed to have influenced New Testament doctrine (resurrection, final judgment, a messiah) were either taught in the Old Testament before the rise of Zoroastrianism or come from later Zoroastrian teachings which first appeared *after* the birth of Christ.

Therefore, we stongly believe if there was any influencing on one by the other, it is Zoroastrianism that has been influenced by the Bible, not the opposite.

Zoroastrianism and Christianity

Although Zoroastrianism has been thought to have exerted an influence over some of the beliefs of Christianity, there is much in Zoroastrianism that is incompatible with Christianity.

The God of Zoroastrianism is similar to the God revealed in the Bible; however, there are some major differences. *Ahura-Mazda* is not an all-powerful God but is only equal in strength to *Angra Mainyu*. They are co-equal and co-eternal.

According to the Bible, God is the only all-powerful Being, with His archenemy, Satan, a created being.

> "'You are My witnesses,' declares the Lord, 'And My servant whom I have chosen, in order that you may know and believe Me, and understand that I am He'" (Isaiah 43:10, NASB). Speaking of Satan, the Scripture says, "You were blameless in your ways from the day you were created, until unrighteousness was found in you" (Ezekiel 28:15, NASB).

Satan is not the opposite of God, for he is neither all-powerful nor eternal. (See our previous volume in this series, *Understanding the Occult*, on the character and abilities of Satan).

Zoroastrianism believes that a person earns favor with God by his good works. There is no answer to the sin problem of mankind, for the difference between a good man and a bad man is considered to be only relative. According to the Bible, there is no one who is good enough on his own to make it to heaven. This is why Jesus Christ had to die on the cross, to solve the problem of sin. The Bible makes this very clear:

> As it is written, There is none righteous, not even one (Romans 3:10, NASB).

> For all have sinned and fall short of the glory of God (Romans 3:23, NASB).

> For the wages of sin is death, but the free gift of God is eternal life in Christ Jesus our Lord (Romans 6:23, NASB).

> For by grace you have been saved through faith, and that not of yourselves, it is the gift of God; not as a result of

works, that no one should boast (Ephesians 2:8, 9, NASB).

He saved us, not on the basis of deeds which we have done in righteousness, but according to His mercy, by the washing of regeneration, and renewing by the Holy Spirit (Titus 3:5, NASB).

The practice of Zoroastrianism involves much that is occultic and superstitious, something resoundingly condemned in the Scripture. The practice of drinking *haoma* (*soma* in India), a hallucinogenic, has become a central rite in Zoroastrian worship.

Any type of involvement in occultic practices is strongly forbidden by the Bible. "There shall not be found among you anyone who makes his son or his daughter pass through the fire, one who interprets omens, or a sorcerer, or one who casts out a spell, or a medium, or a spiritist, or one who calls up the dead. For whoever does these things is detestable to the Lord; and because of these detestable things the Lord your God will drive them out before you" (Deuteronomy 18:10-12, NASB).

Worship in Zoroastrianism is legalistic and impersonal, reflecting the view of its impersonal god, *Ahura-Mazda*. In Christianity, God is to be worshipped personally with all one's heart, since His nature is personal.

Psalm 100 reflects the proper attitude with which to approach the God of the Bible. "Shout joyfully to the Lord, all the earth. Serve the Lord with gladness; come before Him with joyful singing. Know that the Lord Himself is God; it is He who has made us, and not we ourselves; we are His people and the sheep of His pasture. Enter His gates with thanksgiving, and His courts with praise. Give thanks to Him; bless His name. For the Lord is good; His lovingkindness is everlasting, and His faithfulness to all generations" (Psalm 100, NASB).

Zoroastrianism may resemble something of Christianity on the surface, but a close comparison of the two will reveal the contradictory differences between them.

Zoroastrianism Terms

AHURA-MAZDA — The supreme deity, creator of the world, the principle of good.

AMESHA-SPENTA — One of the seven archangels.

ANGRA MAINYU — The evil creator, archenemy of *Ahura-Mazda*.

AVESTA — The sacred scriptures of Zoroastrianism.

DAKHMAS — The towers of silence where the Zoroastrians dispose of their dead by leaving the bodies partially uncovered to be eaten by vultures. This practice keeps the soil and water from being contaminated with dead flesh.

FIRE TEMPLE — The place where fire worship is carried on. An important practice in present-day Zoroastrianism.

GABRAS — The name given Zoroastrians by Muslims. The term denotes an infidel.

VIVEDAT (VENIDAD) — A portion of the *Avesta* containing magic spells and prescriptions for purification.

VOHU MANAH — the archangel also known as *good thought*.

YASNA — The most important portion of the *Avesta*, Zoroastrianism's sacred scripture.

ZEND-AVESTA — A third century A.D. commentary on the Zoroastrian scriptures *(Avesta)* is known as the *Zend*. The combining of the two is called the *Zend-Avesta*.

Zoroastrianism Bibliography

Browne, Lewis, *This Believing World*, New York: MacMillan Company, 1926.

Cavendish, Richard, *The Great Religions*, New York: Arco Publishing Company, 1980.

Hume, Robert E., *The World's Living Religions*, New York: Charles Scribner's Sons, rev. ed., 1959.

Moulton, James Hope, *Early Zoroastrianism*, London: Constable and Company, 1913.

Mueller, Max, ed., *Sacred Books of the East*, Oxford: Krishna Press, 1879-1910.

Rawlings, Maurice, *Life-Wish: Reincarnation: Reality or Hoax*, Nashville: Thomas Nelson Inc., 1981.

Judaism

To Christians, Judaism is unique among world religions. It is to historic Judaism, the Judaism of the Old Testament, that Christianity traces its roots. Christianity does not supplant Old Testament Judaism; it is the fruition of Old Testament Judaism.

One cannot hold to the Bible, Old and New Testaments, as God's one divine revelation without also recognizing and honoring the place God has given historic Judaism. As the apostle Paul recited, these are some of the blessings God has given to the Jewish people:

> ...to whom belongs the adoption as sons and the glory and the covenants and the giving of the Law and the temple service and the promises, whose are the fathers, and from whom is the Christ according to the flesh, who is over all, God blessed forever. Amen (Romans 9:4, 5, NASB).

Judaism has undergone many changes throughout its long history. At times it has been very close to the true God, serving Him in spirit and in deed. At other times it has ranged far from the will of God, forsaking its promises to Him, while He has remained faithful to Israel.

The true God, the Yahweh of the Old Testament, the God of Christianity, is the God of historic Judaism, the same Master, the people of Israel have long occupied a special place in God's divine plan, and Christians should not overlook this rich spiritual heritage.

Although Judaism as a whole has rejected God's greatest

revelation and gift in the Person of Jesus Christ our Lord, Christians cannot deny Judaism's vital contributions to our faith. We should earnestly pray that the physical descendants of Abraham will recognize that their spiritual heritage is also in Abraham and will return to it (see Romans 11:17-24).

History of Judaism

Judaism had its origin when a man named Abram received a divine call from the one true God to leave his idolatrous people in "Ur of the Chaldees" and go to the land of Canaan. This call is recorded in Genesis 12:1-3 (NASB).

> Now the Lord said to Abram,
> Go forth from your country,
> And from your relatives
> And from your father's house,
> To the land which I will show you;
> And I will make you a great nation,
> And I will bless you,
> And make your name great;
> And so you shall be a blessing;
> And I will bless those who bless you,
> And the one who curses you I will curse.
> And in you all the families of the earth shall be blessed.

The promise made to Abram, whose name was later changed to Abraham, included the fact that his descendants would inherit a land which would belong forever to them. This covenant was repeated to Abraham's son Isaac and likewise to Isaac's son Jacob. The family of Jacob, whose name was changed to Israel, migrated to Egypt to escape a severe famine. They were soon enslaved and forced to build mighty cities for the pharaoh. During the years of bondage they continually cried out for a deliverer.

Moses

God eventually raised up a man from among His people to deliver them out of the bondage of Egypt; his name was Moses. Moses led the children of Israel in the exodus from Egypt through the miraculous power of God, which included parting the Red Sea to allow them to escape from the Egyptians. Because of unbelief the people did not immediately enter into the land but wandered in the desert for 40 years. It was during this time of wandering that God gave the Law, including the Ten Commandments, to Moses.*

The Promised Land

Under the leadership of Moses' successor, Joshua, the Jews entered into the promised land but had to conquer the inhabitants before settling down. After Joshua, the nation of Israel was governed by judges for 350 years. During this time they were engaged in numerous battles with the neighboring nations, falling in and out of subjugation to those nations.

After the time of the judges, the Israelites pleaded with God (through the prophet Samuel) for a king to rule them. Although it was not God's desire, He gave them their first king, Saul. Saul did not follow the Lord but almost ruined the nation of Israel. When he died, he had been abandoned by the people and by God.

David, called a man after God's own heart, and divinely appointed to lead the nation, was the second king. He conquered Jerusalem and established it as Israel's capital. David's son Solomon, upon becoming king, built a magnificent temple to the Lord.

During the reign of Solomon, Israel prospered greatly, becoming a leader of nations. Upon the death of Solomon, the nation was divided into two kingdoms, the southern, known as Judea with Jerusalem as its capital, and the northern kingdom of Israel, of which Samaria became the capital.

The Captivity

Both the northern and southern kingdoms were constantly threatened by other nations and each eventually was overcome. The Assyrians conquered the northern kingdom in 721 B.C. and the Babylonians defeated the southern kingdom in 606 B.C. When the southern kingdom was captured, Solomon's temple was destroyed.

---

* See Josh McDowell's previous works, *Evidence that Demands a Verdict* and *More Evidence that Demands a Verdict*, for information on the validity of the Old Testament record and for an affirmation of the validity of miracles.

During the years the southern kingdom was in exile (606 B.C. to 536 B.C.), changes took place with regard to Jewish worship. Since the temple could not be used as a central place of worship, houses of prayer, called synagogues, were established. The teacher of the synagogue, known as the rabbi, grew in importance to the Jewish people and simultaneously the priests lost importance. By the time the Jews returned to their land, the synagogue had become firmly established as the place of worship (but not sacrifice).

The Restoration

During the period of the restoration, the Jews became exposed to Greek culture (Hellenism) when Alexander the Great conquered the world (336-323 B.C.). Upon Alexander's death, the land fell under the rule of the Ptolemies of Egypt. The Hellenic influence was so strong during this time that many Jews no longer understood biblical Hebrew. Aramaic and Greek became the dominant languages in Palestine. During this period the Old Testament was translated into Greek (this text is commonly called the Septuagint, abbreviated as LXX), for the benefit of those Jews who did not read Hebrew.

The Revolt

The people soon became part of the Syrian Kingdom, and when one of the kings, Antiochus IV Epiphanes, tried to suppress the Jewish religion, the people revolted. In 167 B.C. a rebellion led by Judas Maccabaeus resulted in the independence of the Jewish nation, celebrated to this day by the festival of Hanukkah.

The Roman Rule

The independence was short-lived because the Roman general Pompey made Israel a vassal state of Rome in 63 B.C., placing puppet leaders over the people. Rome dominated the people and the land, causing unrest and rebellion among the people. The Roman general Titus destroyed the city of Jerusalem in 70 A.D., scattering the inhabitants. Several rebellions arose after that in an effort to reconquer the land, the last being the Bar Kokhba Rebellion (A.D. 132-135).

Later History

When Christianity became the state religion of the Roman Empire (325 A.D.), the Jews were seen as an accursed race and the center of Jewish life soon moved to Babylonia, a non-Christian country. The Jews did not regain an independent homeland in Israel until 1948 after a long history of persecution which reached its height in the Holocaust of World War II.

The Land

The land of Israel has a very special place in the history of the Jewish people. Leo Trepp comments:

> From the very beginning of history, Jewish destiny has remained inextricably linked to that of the land of Israel. To the Jew, his history starts as Abraham is bidden to migrate to the promised land, for only there can he fulfill himself as the servant and herald of God. The land of Israel always remained the promised land. Only there could Torah be translated freely into the life of an independent nation (Leo Trepp, *Judaism: Development and Life*, Belmont, CA: Dickenson Publishing Company, 1966, pp. 4, 5).

Statement of Faith

One of the great figures in Jewish history was Moses Maimonides, a Spanish Jew who lived in the 12th century A.D. Maimonides, a systematic thinker, tried to condense basic Jewish beliefs into the form of a creed. Although criticized afterward by some, his creed is still followed by the traditional forms of Judaism. The creed is expressed in these 13 basic beliefs:

1. I believe with perfect faith that the Creator, blessed be His Name, is the Creator and Guide of everything that has been created; and He alone has made, does make, and will make all things.

2. I believe with perfect faith that the Creator, blessed be His Name, is One, and that there is no unity in any manner like unto His, and that He alone is our God, who was, and is, and will be.

3. I believe with perfect faith that the Creator, blessed be His Name, is not a body, and that He is free from all the properties of matter, and that He has not any form whatever.

4. I believe with perfect faith that the Creator, blessed be His Name, is the first and the last.

5. I believe with perfect faith that to the Creator, blessed be His Name, and to Him alone, it is right to pray, and that it is not right to pray to any being besides Him.

6. I believe with perfect faith that all the words of the prophets are true.

7. I believe with perfect faith that the prophecy of Moses, our teacher, peace be unto him, was true, and that he was the chief of the prophets, both of those who preceded and of those who followed him.

8. I believe with perfect faith that the whole *Torah*, now in our possession, is the same that was given to Moses, our teacher, peace be unto him.

9. I believe with perfect faith that this Torah will not be changed, and that there will never be any other Law from the Creator, blessed be His Name.

10. I believe with perfect faith that the Creator, blessed be His Name, knows every deed of the children of men, and all their thoughts, as it is said. It is He that fashioned the hearts of them all, that gives heed to all their works.

11. I believe with perfect faith that the Creator, blessed be His Name, rewards those that keep His commandments and punishes those that transgress them.

12. I believe with perfect faith in the coming of the Messiah; and, though he tarry, I will wait daily for his coming.

13. I believe with perfect faith that there will be a revival of the dead at the time when it shall please the Creator, blessed be His Name, and exalted be His Fame for ever and ever.

For Thy salvation I hope, O Lord.

Jewish Holy Days

The cycle of Jewish holy days is called the sacred round. Based on the ancient Jewish calendar, these holy days serve to remind Jews regularly of significant historical events in which God displayed his covenant with them and to give them regular opportunity to display their commitment to God.

The Sabbath

This is a holy day of rest, in commemoration of God's completed work of creation and in His later liberation of the Israelites from the bondage in Egypt. It is a day of joy and thanksgiving to God for His many blessings.

Passover

Passover *(Pessah)*, the festival of spring is celebrated one month after Purim. It constitutes the beginning of the time of harvest; therefore, it is a time of celebration. However, there is a deeper reason for the people to observe this holiday, as the Scriptures plainly reveal. This feast celebrates the deliverance of the children of Israel from the bondage of Egypt.

The story of the Passover is given in Exodus 12: God sent the final plague on the Egyptians; the death of the firstborn. However, those who put blood on their doorposts were passed over by the angel of death. This plague was instrumental in convincing the pharaoh to allow the children of Israel to leave. Consequently, it is to be celebrated as a permanent memorial by the Jewish people. Deuteronomy 16:1-4 (NASB) tells how it is to be observed:

> Observe the month of Abib and celebrate the Passover to the Lord your God, for in the month of Abib the Lord your God brought you out of Egypt by night.
>
> And you shall sacrifice the Passover to the Lord your God from the flock and the herd, in the place where the Lord chooses to establish His name.
>
> You shall not eat leavened bread with it; seven days you shall eat with it unleavened bread, the bread of affliction (for you came out of the land of Egypt in haste), in order that you may remember all the days of your life the day when you came out of the land of Egypt.
>
> For seven days no leaven shall be seen with you in all your territory, and none of the flesh which you sacrifice on the evening of the first day shall remain overnight until morning.

Shabuot

Shabuot, the feast of weeks, comes seven weeks after the Passover. Shabuot commemorates the giving of the Ten Commandments. During ancient times the farmer would bring his firstfruits to the temple on Shabuot and offer them to God. The day is also celebrated by the reading of the Ten Commandments and the recitation of the book of Ruth.

Rosh Hashanah

Rosh Hashanah literally means "head of the year." It is the Jewish New Year, celebrated on the first two days of the month of Tishai (September-October). It is a solemn day of reflection on both the deeds of the past year and the hopes of the upcoming one.

The ram's horn (*shofar*) is sounded in daily worship for an entire month before Rosh Hashanah, calling the people to repentance. Moses Maimonides, the great Jewish theologian and philosopher, explained the message of the day:

> Wake up, ye sleepers, from your sleep; and ye that are in a daze, arouse yourselves from your stupor. Reflect on your actions and return in repentance. Remember your Creator. Be not as those who forget truth in their chase after shadows, wasting their year wholly in vanities which neither help nor bring deliverance. Look into your soul, and mend your ways and deeds. Let everyone forsake his evil ways and worthless thoughts (*Teshubah* 3, 4).

Yom Kippur

Yom Kippur is the holiest day of the year, the day of atonement. It is celebrated ten days after Rosh Hashanah and is devoted to confession of sins and reconciliation with God. Problems with enemies must be reconciled before one can be right with God, and forgiving and forgetting is the order of the day. The day is spent without touching food or drink, the mind being devoted to God on this holiest of days. During this day of confession of sin and fasting, the following passage from Isaiah is read:

> Is it a fast like this which I choose, a day for a man to humble himself? Is it for bowing one's head like a reed, and for spreading out sackcloth and ashes as a bed? Will you call this a fast, even an acceptable day to the Lord? Is this not the fast which I chose, to loosen the bonds of wickedness, to undo the bands of the yoke, and to let the oppressed go free, and break every yoke? Is it not to divide your bread with the hungry, and bring the homeless poor into the house, when you see the naked, to cover him; and not to hide yourself from your own flesh? (Isaiah 58:5-7, NASB)

Yom Kippur has a long Jewish and biblical tradition and is the most important Jewish holy day. Usually even liberal or non-practicing Jews consider the day holy and devote themselves to contrite contemplation and prayer on this day.

Milton Steinberg effectively summarizes the Jewish concept of Yom Kippur:

> ...Yom Kippur, the day of Atonement, a solemn white fast, during which from dusk to dusk the faithful partake of neither food nor drink in token of penitence, but through prayer and confession scrutinize their lives, abjure their evil-doing, and seek regeneration, a returning to God and goodness (Milton Steinberg, *Basic Judaism*, New York: Harcourt Brace Jovanovich, 1947, 1975, pp. 130, 131).

Sukkoth

Sukkoth is the feast of tabernacles, or booths. This festival, which commemorates the ingathering of the harvest, is one of the three pilgrim feasts in ancient times where yearly trips were made to the Temple of Jerusalem. It is known as the feast of booths because the people lived in tabernacles, or temporary shelters, during its duration (Exodus 34:18-26). In modern times the people, for the most part, only take their meals in these tabernacles rather than living in them for the duration of the feast.

Hanukkah

Hanukkah, observed for eight days in midwinter, is the only major feast that does not have its source in the Bible. The feast is based upon the story of the Maccabees, recorded in the Apocrypha. When Antiochus IV Epiphanes in 167 B.C. introduced the worship of the Greek gods as the state religion, a small group of Jews led by Judas Maccabee staged a revolt.

Antiochus, who, among other things desecrated the temple by slaughtering a pig in the Holy of Holies, was finally overthrown and freedom of religion returned to the land. Hanukkah is celebrated in observance of the heroic acts of the Maccabees.

The eight-branched candlestick, the Menorah, is integral to Hanukkah worship and commemorates a miracle that took place when the temple was cleansed from the idolatrous acts of Antiochus IV Epiphanes. The tradition states that only enough holy oil was found in the temple to light the lamp for one night. However, because of the providence of God and as a sign that He blessed the Jewish cleansing and rededication of the temple, God miraculously kept the lamp burning for eight days and nights.

Since Hanukkah is celebrated near the Christian Christmas holiday, it has borrowed some ideas from Christmas, including the giving of gifts (traditionally one to each child each of the eight nights), and family gatherings. Especially among non-practicing and reform (liberal) Jews, Hanukkah is a very important holiday.

The Three Branches of Judaism

Very simply stated, modern-day Judaism can be divided into three groups: Orthodox, Conservative and Reform.

Orthodox

Orthodox Judaism designates the traditionalists who are united in their upholding of the Law. The *Encyclopedia of Jewish Religion* says:

> Though Orthodoxy is widely diversified among its many religious groupings and nuances of belief and practice, all Orthodox Jews are united in their belief in the historical event of revelation at Sinai, as described in the Torah; in their acceptance of the Divine Law, in its Written and Oral forms, as immutable and binding for all times; in their acknowledgment of the authority of duly qualified rabbis — who themselves recognize the validity of the Talmud and all other traditional sources of the Halakhah — to interpret and administer Jewish Law (*Encyclopedia of Jewish Religion*, New York: Holt, Rhinehart and Winston, 1966, p. 293).

Orthodox Judaism observes most of the traditional dietary and ceremonial laws of Judaism. It adheres to the inspiration of the Old Testament [although greater authority is given the Torah (Law), the first five books, than to the rest].

Conservative

Conservative Judaism is sort of a happy medium between Orthodox and Reform Judaism. Founded in the 19th century, the Conservative movement quickly gained strength in both Germany and the United States.

In 1918, six months after the Balfour Declaration, the Conservative movement announced:

> We hold that Jewish people are and of right ought to be at home in all lands. Israel, like every other religious communion, has the right to live and assert its message in any part of the world. We are opposed to the idea that Palestine should be considered *the home-land* of the Jews. Jews in America are part of the American nation.
>
> The ideal of the Jew is not the establishment of a Jewish state—not the reassertion of Jewish nationality which has long been outgrown. We believe that our survival as a people is dependent upon the assertion and the maintenance of our historic religious role and not upon the acceptance of Palestine as a home-land of the Jewish people. The mission of the Jew is to witness to God all over the world.

Reform

Reform Judaism is the liberal wing of Judaism. Leo Trepp traces its development:

> Abraham Geiger (1810-1874) stands out as the towering genius of Reform Judaism, and is essentially its founder. To him the scientific man cannot accept revelation, for science offers no proof of any revelation. Mendelssohn had seen Judaism as *revealed* law; Geiger rejected this idea, as he equally rejected any revealed doctrines. He refuted the hope for a return to the Land, for the land of citizenship is the land of the Jew. This was an attack on the validity of Torah, of Mitzvot, and of the Land. What remained, then, was the deep-seated sense of kinship with the Jewish *people* (a feeling of which Geiger himself may have been unaware, but which kept him from suggesting the dissolution of Judaism in favor of a general religion of ethical conduct).
>
> Thus, Torah to him becomes a source of ethics, performance of Mitzvot becomes a matter of individual decision, but not binding, the *Talmud* and *Shulhan Arukh* have no power of commitment, and the messianic hope has been fulfilled in Jewish Emancipation. However, the genius of the Jewish people as teachers of ethics was strongly emphasized. The Hebrew language of prayer was to be retained in part, at least, for its emotional appeal. Education, sermon, and worship now were to form Torah in this new interpretation, and Mitzvot were to be understood as the missionary ideal of spreading ethics throughout the world. For these the Jew must live. The effect of Geiger's Reform Judaism was to be strongly felt, especially in America (Leo Trepp, *op. cit.*, pp. 50, 51).

Reform Judaism is so culture- and race-oriented that it easily can neglect the spiritual and religious side of Jewish life. Rather than assuming that the religious life produces and molds the culture, Reform Judaism assumes that the cultural and racial heritage of the Jews produced and molded the religious life. While belief and doctrine may be changeable or even dispensable, the cultural history of the race is vital to any continuation of Jewishness. There is little concensus on doctrinal or religious belief in Reform Judaism.

Doctrine

Judaism and the Messiah

While Christianity recognizes that the promise of a personal, spiritual savior is the core of biblical revelation, Judaism has long vacillated in its concept of messiahship. That Jesus Christ, the true Messiah predicted in God's Word, would be rejected by the Jews of the first century shows that even at that time there was divergence of opinion on the meaning and authority of messianic passages in Scripture. *

In the course of Jewish history the meaning of the Messiah had undergone changes. Originally it was believed that God would send His special messenger, delivering Israel from her oppressors and instituting peace and freedom. However, today, any idea of a personal messiah has been all but abandoned by the majority of Jews. It has been substituted with the hope of a messianic age characterized by truth and justice.

Within the history of Judaism, from the time of Jesus of Nazareth until Moses Hayyim Luzatto (died A.D. 1747), there have been at least 34 different prominent Jews who have claimed to be the Messiah (James Hastings, *Encyclopedia of Religion and Ethics*, Vol. 8, New York and London: Scribner's and T. & T. Clark, 1919, pp. 581-588).

Carrying on one Jewish tradition, most of these self-

---

* For a discussion of Old Testament prophecies concerning the messiahship of Jesus, see Josh McDowell's *Evidence that Demands a Verdict*, pp. 144 ff.

proclaimed messiahs promised salvation from political, economic and cultural oppression, rather than spiritual salvation. Only Jesus of Nazareth perfectly fulfilled the Old Testament passages concerning the Messiah and only He validated His claims by His victory over death, displayed in His glorious resurrection from the dead (Acts 2:22-36).

God

The orthodox Jewish concept of God is based upon the Old Testament. The Hebrew scholar Samuel Sandmel summarizes the biblical teaching:

> The heritage from the Bible included a number of significant components about the Deity. God was not a physical being: He was intangible and invisible. He was the Creator and Ruler, indeed, the Judge of the World. He and He alone was truly God; the deities worshipped by peoples other than Israel were not God. Idols were powerless and futile; they were unworthy of worship; and indeed, to worship what was not God was a gross and sinful disrespect of Him.
>
> Scripture contains an abundance of divine terms: Elohim, El, El Elyon, Shaddai. Insofar as God might be thought of as having a name, that name was Yahve. But so holy and awesome was He that His name Yahve itself had force and power, and it was unbecoming or even sinful for men to pronounce it, as was expressed in the words "You shall not take the name of Yahve your God in vain" (Exod. 20:7, Deut. 5:11). Only the High Priest might pronounce it, and only on one day in the year, that on the Day of Atonement.
>
> God was, as it were, above and over the world. His dwelling was in heaven. At high moments, such as at Sinai, He had descended to reveal Himself. Accordingly, He was both in the world and also over and above it. He had very early revealed Himself to the patriarchs; He had later revealed Himself to the prophets. To some of these prophets, such as Zechariah, He had disclosed His divine will and intention by sending an angel to bring His desires from the distance to earth. Apart from sending an angel, He could, and did, pour His "holy" spirit onto selected men. In heaven there were a host of beings, subordinate to Him, who constituted His heavenly council. Among these was Satan who could with divine consent test a man such as Job; a lying spirit who could on occasion delude a presumptuous king or prophet (Samuel Sandmel, *Judaism and Christian Beginnings*, London: Oxford University Press, 1978, pp. 168, 169).

The sacred scriptures of Judaism consist of documents arranged in three groups known as the Law, the Prophets, and the Writings. These books were originally written in Hebrew, except for parts of Daniel and Ezra and a verse in Jeremiah which were composed in Aramaic. These books are synonymous with the 39 books of Christianity's Old Testament. Their composition was over a period of some one thousand years, from 1400-400 B.C.

The Jews do not hold each part of their writings in equal importance. *The Law*, the Torah, is the most authoritative, followed by *the Prophets*, which have lesser authority, and lastly *the Writings*.

Salvation in Judaism

Judaism, while admitting the existence of sin, its abhorrence by God, and the necessity for atonement, has not developed a system of salvation teaching as found in Christianity. Atonement is accomplished by sacrifices, penitence, good deeds and a little of God's grace. No concept of substitutionary atonement (as in Christianity in the Person of Jesus Christ) exists.

Scholar Michael Wyschogrod explains the difference:

A Jew who believes that man is justified by works of the law would hold the belief that man can demand only strict justice from God, nothing more. Such a man would say to God: "Give me what I deserve, neither more nor less; I do not need your mercy, only your strict justice."

If there are Jews who approach God in this spirit, I have never met nor heard of them. In the morning liturgy that Jews recite daily, we find the following: "Master of all worlds: It is not on account of our own righteousness that we offer our supplications before thee, but on account of thy great compassion. What are we? What is our life? What is our goodness? What is our virtue? What is our help? What our strength? What our might?"

The believing Jew is fully aware that if he were to be judged strictly according to his deeds by the standards of justice and without mercy, he would be doomed. He realizes that without the mercy of God there is no hope for him and that he is therefore justified—if by "justified" we mean that he avoids the direst of divine punishments—not by the merit of his works as commanded in the Torah, but by the gratuitous mercy of God who saves man in spite of the fact that man does not deserve it (Tanenbaum, Wilson, and Rudin, eds., *Evangelicals and Jews in Conversation on Scripture, Theology, and History*, Grand Rapids, MI: Baker Book House, 1978, pp. 47, 48).

So then, Jews do believe in the mercy of God but they do not believe in any substitutionary atonement that once and for all time cleanses them from all sin. Contrast this with the great passage of assurance in Hebrews 7:22-28 (NASB):

> So much the more also Jesus has become the guarantee of a better covenant. And the former priests, on the one hand, existed in greater numbers, because they were prevented by death from continuing, but He, on the other hand, because He abides forever, holds His priesthood permanently. Hence, also, He is able to save forever those who draw near to God through Him, since He always lives to make intercession for them. For it was fitting that we should have such a high priest, holy, innocent, undefiled, separated from sinners and exalted above the heavens; who does not need daily, like those high priests, to offer up sacrifices, first for His own sins, and then for the sins of the people, because this He did once for all when He offered up Himself. For the Law appoints men as high priests who are weak, but the work of the oath, which came after the Law, appoints a Son, made perfect forever.

Original Sin

Judaism holds no concept of original sin. According to Christian belief, all human beings are born into the world with a sinful nature because of the transgression of Adam (Romans 5:12-21). Judaism's emphasis is not on original sin but original virtue and righteousness. Although Judaism acknowledges that man does commit acts of sin, there is not a sense of man being totally depraved or unworthy as is found in Christian theology.

Atonement for sin is achieved by works of righteousness, which include repentance, prayer and the performing of good deeds. There is no need for a savior, as is emphasized in Christianity.

J.H. Hertz writes:

> Note that the initiative in atonement is with the sinner (Ezekiel 18:31). He cleanses himself on the Day of Atonement by fearless self-examination, open confession, and the resolve not to repeat the transgressions of the past year. When our

Heavenly Father sees the abasement of the penitent sinner, He sprinkles, as it were, the clean waters of pardon and forgiveness upon him. And again: On the Day of Atonement the Israelites resemble the angels, without human wants, without sins, linked together in love and peace. It is the only day of the year on which the accuser Satan is silenced before the throne of Glory, and even becomes the defender of Israel....The closing prayer (on the Day of Atonement) begins: "Thou givest a hand to transgressors, and Thy right hand is stretched out to receive the penitent. Thou hast taught us to make confession unto Thee of all our sins, in order that we may cease from the violence of our hands and may return unto Thee who delightest in the repentance of the wicked." These words contain what has been called "the Jewish doctrine of salvation" (J. H. Hertz, *The Pentateuch and the Haftorahs*, London: Socino Press, 1938, p. 523 f).

A Common Heritage

Although there are marked differences in many areas of belief and practice between Judaism and Christianity, there is a common heritage that both religions share. The Jewish writer, Pinchas Lapide, comments:

We Jews and Christians are joined in brotherhood at the deepest level, so deep in fact that we have overlooked it and missed the forest of brotherhood for the trees of theology. We have an intellectual and spiritual kinship which goes deeper than dogmatics, hermeneutics, and exegesis. We are brothers in a manifold "elective affinity"

— in the belief in one God our Father,
— in the hope of His salvation,
— in ignorance of His ways,
— in humility before His omnipotence,
— in the knowledge that we belong to Him, not He to us,
— in love and reverence for God,
— in doubt about our wavering fidelity,
— in the paradox that we are dust and yet the image of God,
— in the consciousness that God wants us as partners in the sanctification of the world,
— in the condemnation of arrogant relegous chauvinism,
— in the conviction that love of God is crippled without love of neighbor,
— in the knowledge that all speech about God must remain in a stammering on our way to Him (Pinchas

Lapide *Israelis, Jews and Jesus*, Garden City, NJ: Doubleday and Company, 1979, p. 2).

The book of Galatians gives us God's view of Jews and Gentiles today. Chapter 3 shows forcefully that God's blessings on the Jews were a means of showing His grace, which was fully expressed in the sacrifice of His son, Jesus Christ, on the cross for the sins of all, Jewish or Gentile. The gospel was preached beforehand to Abraham, the Father of the Jews (5:8) and was given to the Gentiles in Jesus Christ (5:14).

The heritage of the Old Testament, preserved for all mankind by the Jews, points all of us, Jewish or Gentile, to Jesus Christ (5:22-24). Each man, whether of Jewish or Gentile heritage, must come to God through Jesus Christ. There is no other way to true peace with God. As Galatians 3: 26-29 concludes, "For you are all sons of God through faith in Christ Jesus. For all of you who were baptized into Christ have clothed yourselves with Christ. There is neither Jew nor Greek, there is neither slave nor free man, there is neither male nor female; for you are all one in Christ Jesus. And if you belong to Christ, then you are Abraham's offspring, heirs according to promise."

Judaistic Terms

DIASPORA—The dispersion of the Jews after the Babylonian Captivity.

GEMARAH—The commentary based upon the Mishnah.

HANNUKAH—The feast of dedication celebrating the Maccabean victory in 167 B.C.

MIDRASH—A commentary of the Hebrew scriptures, especially the Torah.

MISHNAH—Oral law in general to be distinguished from scripture.

PASSOVER—An annual feast commemorating the deliverance of the firstborn in Egypt when the angel of death took all those who did not have blood on the doorpost.

PENTATEUCH—The first five books of the Old Testament.

PENTECOST—The feast of weeks observed fifty days after the Passover. Also called Shabuoth.

PURIM—The feast commemorating Esther's intervention on behalf of the Jews when they were in Persia.

ROSH HASHANAH—The Jewish New Year.

SEDER—The festival held in Jewish homes on the first night of the Passover commemorating the Exodus from Egypt.

SUKKOTH—The feast of tabernacles celebrating the harvest.

TORAH—Refers to the first five books of the Old Testament (The Law). It also can refer to the entire corpus of the Jewish law.

SHOPHAR—The ram's horn that is blown during services on Rosh Hashanah.

TALMUD—The Jewish library of oral law and tradition consisting of Mishnah and Gemara.

Judaism Bibliography

Encyclopedia of Jewish Religion, New York: Holt, Rhinehart and Winston, 1966.

Hastings, James, *Encyclopedia of Religion and Ethics, Vol. 8*, New York and London: Scribner's and T. & T. Clark, 1919.

Hertz, J. H., *The Pentateuch and the Haftorahs*, London: Socino Press, 1938.

Lapide, Pinchas, *Israelis, Jews and Jesus*, Garden City, NJ: Doubleday and Company, 1979.

Sandmel, Samuel, *Judaism and Christian Beginnings*, London: Oxford University Press, 1978.

Steinberg, Milton, *Basic Judaism*, New York: Harcourt Brace Jovanovich, 1947, 1975.

Tanenbaum, Marc, and Wilson, and Rudin, eds., *Evangelicals and Jews in Conversation on Scripture, Theology, and History*, Grand Rapids, MI: Baker Book House, 1978.

Trepp, Leo, *Judaism: Development and Life*, Belmont, CA: Dickenson Publishing Company, 1966.

Islam

I n recent years, Islam has been in the spotlight because of the heightened tension in the Middle East. This has served to put its culture under the microscope of world attention. Islam is indeed a major part of Middle Eastern culture, but it is much more.

The Muslim (var. sp.: Moslem) faith is a major driving force in the lives of many of the nations in the Middle East, West Asia and North Africa. The impact of this faith on the world has been increasing steadily. Today, Islam is the fastest-growing religion in the world. In large part, the Arab-Israel tension can be traced back to the Islam-Judaism conflict.

Not only does Islam collectively wield a strong sword in world conflict as Muslims threaten war with Israel, but Islamic sects also threaten even greater unrest in the fragile Middle East and could be catalysts for greater conflict. Right-wing Islamic fundamentalists were responsible for both the takeover of Iran and the assassination of Egyptian President Anwar el-Sadat.

The vast majority of Muslims, however, are not of this militant variety. The contrast between the moderate and progressive Islam of Egypt and the fundamentalistic and reactionary Islam of Iran is marked. Islam has had a great deal of positive impact on many countries where it is a strong force. But positive influence is no reason to follow any religion with one's life-commitment. One must examine the teachings of Islam along with one's faith and ascertain what is true and why.

The very impact of Islam in history also makes it worthy of study. Sir Norman Anderson capsulizes it this way:

> The religion of Islam is one of the outstanding phenomena of history. Within a century of the death of its founder, the Muslim Empire stretched from Southern France through Spain, North Africa, the Levant and Central Asia to the confines of China; and, although Islam has since been virtually expelled from Western Europe and has lost much of its political power elsewhere, it has from time to time made notable advances in Eastern Europe, in Africa, in India, and in Southeast Asia. Today it extends from the Atlantic to the Philippines and numbers some three hundred million adherents drawn from races as different as the European from the Bantu, and the Aryan Indian from the primitive Philippine tribesmen; yet it is still possible to speak of the "World of Islam" (Sir Norman Anderson, ed., *The World's Religions*, Grand Rapids, MI: William B. Eerdmans Publishing Company, 1976, p. 52).

Today, there are an estimated 450 million members of Islam which dominate more than three dozen countries on three continents. The word *Islam* is a noun which is formed from the Arabic verb meaning "to submit, surrender or commit oneself." *Islam* means submission or surrender, and with the translation comes the idea of action, not simple stagnation. The very act of submissive commitment is at the heart of Islam, not simply a passive acceptance and surrender to doctrine. *Muslim*, another noun form of the same verb, means "the one who submits."

History of Islam

The early history of Islam revolves around one central figure, Muhammad (var. sp.: Muhammed, Mohammed). Although the teaching of Islam is an interesting mixture of different religions, the origin of the faith is found historically in the one person of Muhammad.

Muhammad

Born around 570 A.D. in the city of Mecca in Arabia,

Muhammad's father died before his birth. His mother died when he was six. He was raised first by his grandfather and later by his uncle. Muhammad's early background is not well known. Some scholars believe he came from a well-respected family, but this is not certain. What is clear is that he was of the Hashimite clan of the *Al Qu'raysh* tribe. At the age of 25, he married a wealthy 40-year-old widow named Khadijah. Of his life Anderson relates:

> There is evidence in a tradition which can scarcely have been fabricated that Muhammad suffered in early life from fits. Be that as it may, the adult Muhammad soon showed signs of a markedly religious disposition. He would retire to caves for seclusion and meditation; he frequently practiced fasting; and he was prone to dreams. Profoundly dissatisfied with the polytheism and crude superstitions of his native Mecca, he appears to have become passionately convinced of the existence and transcendence of one true God. How much of this conviction he owed to Christianity or Judaism it seems impossible to determine. Monophysite Christianity was at that time widely spread in the Arab Kingdom of Ghassan; the Byzantine Church was represented by hermits dotted about the Hijaz with whom he may well have come into contact; the Nestorians were established at al Hira and in Persia; and the Jews were strongly represented in al Madina, the Yemen and elsewhere. There can be no manner of doubt, moreover, that at some period of his life he absorbed much teaching from Talmudic sources and had contact with some form of Christianity; and it seems overwhelmingly probable that his early adoption of monotheism can be traced to one or both of these influences (*Ibid.*, p. 54).

The character of Muhammad was quite a mosaic, as Anderson summarizes:

> For the rest, his character seems, like that of many another, to have been a strange mixture. He was a poet rather than a theologian: a master improvisor rather than a systematic thinker. That he was in the main simple in his tastes and kindly in his disposition there can be no doubt; he was generous, resolute, genial and astute: a shrewd judge and a born leader of men. He could, however, be cruel and vindictive to his enemies; he could stoop to assassination; and he was undeniably sensual (*Ibid.*, p. 60).

Robert Payne also brings this out in his book, *The Holy Sword:*

It is worthwhile to pause for a moment before the quite
astonishing polarity of Muhammad's mind. Violence and
gentleness were at war within him. Sometimes he gives the
appearance of living simultaneously in two worlds, at one
and the same moment seeing the world about to be destroyed
by the flames of God and in a state of divine peace; and he
seems to hold these opposing visions only at the cost of an
overwhelming sense of strain. Sometimes the spring snaps,
and we see him gazing with a look of bafflement at the world
around him, which is neither the world in flames nor the
world in a state of blessedness, but the ordinary day-to-day
world in which he was rarely at home (Robert Payne, *The
Holy Sword*, New York: Collier Books, 1962, p. 84).

The Call

As Muhammad grew, his views changed. He came to
believe in only one God, Allah, a monotheistic faith. He
rejected the idolatrous polytheism of those around him.
By the age of 40, the now religious Muhammad had his
first vision. These revelations are what are recorded in the
Qur'an (Koran).

Muhammad was at first unsure of the source of these
visions, whether divine or demonic. His wife, Khadijah,
encouraged him to believe they had come from God. Later
she became his first convert. However, his most important early convert was a wealthy merchant named Abu
Bakr, who eventually became one of his successors.

The Cambrige History of Islam comments on
Muhammad's revelations:

Either in the course of the visions or shortly afterwards,
Muhammad began to receive "messages" or "revelations"
from God. Sometimes he may have heard the words being
spoken to him, but for the most part he seems simply to have
"found them in his heart." Whatever the precise "manner of
revelation" — and several different "manners" were listed by
Muslim scholars — the important point is that the message
was not the product of Muhammad's conscious mind. He
believed that he could easily distinguish between his own
thinking and these revelations.

The messages which thus came to Muhammad from
beyond his conscious mind were at first fairly short, and
consisted of short verses ending in a common rhyme or
assonance. They were committed to memory by Muhammad
and his followers, and recited as part of their common

worship. Muhammad continued to receive the messages at intervals until his death. In his closing years the revelations tended to be longer, to have much longer verses and to deal with the affairs of the community of Muslims at Medina. All, or at least many, of the revelations were probably written down during Muhammad's lifetime by his secretaries (P.M. Holt, ed., *The Cambridge History of Islam*, Vol. II, London: Cambridge University Press, 1970, pp. 31, 32).

Alfred Guillaume states:

Now if we look at the accounts of his call, as recorded by the early biographers, some very interesting parallels with Hebrew prophets come to light. They say that it was his habit to leave the haunts of men and retire to the mountains to give himself up to prayer and meditation. One night as he was asleep the angel Gabriel came to him with a piece of silk brocade whereon words were written, and said "Recite!" He answered "What shall I recite?" The order was repeated three times, while he felt continually increasing physical pressure, until the angel said:

> Recite in the name of thy Lord who created
> Man from blood coagulated.
> Recite! Thy Lord is wondrous kind
> Who by the pen has taught mankind
> Things they knew not (being blind).

When he woke these words seemed to be written on his heart (or, as we should say, impressed idelibly on his mind). Then the thought came to him that he must be a *sha'ir* or possessed, he who had so hated such people that he could not bear the sight of them; and he could not tolerate the thought that his tribesmen would regard him as one of them — as in fact they afterwards did. Thereupon he left the place with the intention of throwing himself over a precipice. But while on his way he heard a voice from heaven hailing him as the Apostle of God, and lifting up his eyes he saw a figure astride the horizon which turned him from his purpose and kept him rooted to the spot. And there he remained long after his anxious wife's messengers had returned to report that they could not find him (Alfred Guillaume, *Islam*, London: Penguin Books, 1954, pp. 28, 29).

Sir Norman Anderson discusses how Muhammad at first thought he was possessed by the demons, or Jinn, as they were called, but later dismissed the idea:

It seems, however, that Muhammed himself was at first doubtful of the source of these revelations, fearing that he was possessed by one of the Jinn, or sprites, as was commonly believed to be the case with Arab poets and soothsayers. But Khadijah and others reassured him, and he soon began to propound divine revelations with increasing frequency (Anderson, *op. cit.*, p. 55).

These visions mark the start of Muhammed's prophetic call by Allah. Muhammed received these visions during the following 22 years, until his death in 632 A.D.

The Hijira

The new faith encountered opposition in Muhammed's home town of Mecca. Because of his rejection in Mecca and the ostracism of his views, Muhammed and followers withdrew to the city now known as *Medina*, which means in full, "City of the Prophet," renamed from its original *Yathrib*.

The Hijira, which means "flight," marks the turning point in Islam. All Islamic calendars mark this date, July 16, 622, as their beginning. Thus, 630 A.D. would be 8 A.H. (in the year of the Hijira).

In his early years in Medina, Muhammed was sympathetic to both the Jews and Christians as well. But they rejected him and his teaching. Upon that rejection, Muhammed turned from Jerusalem as the center of worship of Islam, to Mecca, where the famous black stone Ka'aba was enshrined. Muhammed denounced all the idols which surrounded the Ka'aba and declared it was a shrine for the one true God, Allah.

With this new emphasis on Mecca, Muhammed realized he must soon return to his home. The rejected prophet did return in triumph, conquering the city.

John B. Noss details some of Muhammed's actions upon his return to Mecca:

> One of his first acts was to go reverently to the Ka'aba; yet he showed no signs of yielding to the ancient Meccan polytheism. After honoring the Black Stone and riding seven times around the shrine, he ordered the destruction of the idols within it and the scraping of the paintings of Abraham and the angels from the walls. He sanctioned the use of the well Zamzam and restored the boundary pillars defining the sacred territory around Mecca. Thenceforth no Muslim would have cause to hesitate about going on a pilgrimage to the ancient holy city.

Muhammed now made sure of his political and prophetic ascendency in Arabia. Active opponents near at hand were conquered by the sword, and tribes far away were invited sternly to send delegations offering their allegience. Before his sudden death in 632 he knew he was well on the way to unifying the Arab tribes under a theocracy governed by the will of God (John B. Noss, *Man's Religions*, New York: MacMillan Publishing Company Inc., 1974, p. 517).

Between the return to Mecca and Muhammad's death, the prophet zealously and militantly propagated Islam, and the new faith quickly spread throughout the area.

After Muhammad's Death

When Muhammad died he had not written a will instructing the leadership in Islam about determining his successor. Sir Norman Anderson comments:

> Muhammad died, according to the best-supported view, without having designated any successor (Khalifa or Caliph). As the last and greatest of the Prophets he could not, of course, be replaced. But the community he had founded was a theocracy with no distinction between Church and State, and someone must clearly succeed, not to give but to enforce the law, to lead in war and to guide in peace. It was common ground, therefore, that a Caliph must be appointed: and in the event 'Umar ibn al Khattab (himself the second Caliph) succeeded in rushing the election of the aged Abu Bakr, one of the very first believers. But the question of the Caliphate was to cause more divisions and bloodshed than any other issue in Islam, and almost from the first three rival parties, in embryo at least, can be discerned. There were the Companions of the Prophet, who believed in the eligibility of any suitable "Early Believer" of the tribe of Quraysh; there was the aristocracy of Mecca, who wished to capture the Caliphate for the family of Umayya; and there were the "legitimists," who believed that no election was needed, but that 'Ali, the cousin and son-in-law of the Prophet, had been divinely designated as his successor (Anderson, *op cit.*, p. 64).

Abu Bakr died less than two years after his designation as Caliph. Upon his death, 'Umar became successor, and under him the borders of the Islamic empire were considerably expanded.

Eventually a power struggle developed as different factions believed their own methods of establishing a successor were better than their rivals. The major eruption came between those who believed the Caliph should be elected by the Islamic leadership and those who believed the successor should be hereditary, through 'Ali, Muhammad's son-in-law, married to his only daughter, *Fatima*. This struggle, along with others, produced the main body of Islam known as the Sunnis (followers of the prophet's way) as well as numerous sects.

The Sunnis

Along with the Caliphate controversy, conflict raged on another front, that of law and theology. Through this conflict eventually four recognized, orthodox schools of Islamic thought emerged. All four schools accepted the *Qur'an* (Koran), the *Sunna*, or the practice of the Prophet as expressed in the *Hadith* (traditions) and the four bases of Islamic Law *(Shari'a)*: the *Qur'an*, the *Hadith*, the *Ij'ma'* (consensus of the Muslim community) and the *Q'yas* (use of analogical reason). These four groups came to be called the Sunnis.

Noss explains:

> The rapid expansion of Islam confronted Muslims with other crucial, and even more complex, decisions concerning Muslim behavior. Situations early appeared in areas outside of Arabia where the injunctions of the Qur'an proved either insufficient or inapplicable. The natural first step in these cases was to appeal to the *sunna* (the behavior or practice) of Muhammad in Medina or to the Hadith that reported his spoken decisions or judgments. In the event that this proved inconclusive, the next step was to ask what the sunna and/or consensus of opinion *(Ijmā)* of the Medina community was, in or shortly after the time of Muhammad. If no light was yet obtainable, the only recourse was either to draw an analogy *(Qiyās)* from the principles embodied in the Qur'an or in Medinan precedents and then apply it, or to follow the consensus of opinion of the local Muslim community as crystallized and expressed by its Qur'anic authorities.
>
> The Muslims who took this way of solving their behavioral problems were, and are to this day, called Sunnites (Noss, *op. cit.*, p. 530).

The Majority of Islam today is Sunni.

The Shi'a

The fourth Caliph to follow Muhammed was an early convert and also his son-in-law, *'Ali.* He was eventually murdered by *Mu'awiya*, who claimed the Caliphate for himself.

The tragedy that befell the House of 'Ali, beginning with the murder of 'Ali himself and including the deaths of his two sons, grandsons of Muhammad, has haunted the lives of "the party *(Shi'a)* of 'Ali." They have brooded upon these dark happenings down the years as Christians do upon the death of Jesus. A major heretical group, they have drawn the censure and yet also have had the sympathy of the Sunnis and Sufis. They were among the sects whose radical elements al-Ghazali attacked as guilty of resting their claims on false grounds and sinfully dividing Islam. And yet, although agreeing with this indictment, the Muslim world at large has suppressed its annoyance at them, because their movement goes back to the very beginnings of Islam and has a kind of perverse justification, even in orthodox eyes. Their critics agree that there is little sense in it, yet it has an appeal of its own.

The partisans of 'Ali only gradually worked out the final claims made by the various Shi'ite sects. In the beginning there was simply the assertion—which as events unfolded became more and more heated—that only Muhammad's direct descendants, no others, could be legitimate caliphs; only they should have been given first place in the leadership of Islam. This "legitimism" could be called their political and dynastic claim, and at first this seems to have been all that they were interested in claiming. But this was not enough for adherents of their cause in Iraq, who over the years developed the religious theory, perhaps as an effect of Christian theories about God being in Christ, that every legitimate leader of the 'Alids, beginning with 'Ali, was an *imam mahdi*, a divinely appointed and supernaturally guided spiritual leader, endowed by Allah with special knowledge and insight—an assertion that the main body of Muslims, significantly enough called *ghuluw*, "exaggeration," rather than heresy (Noss, *op. cit.*, p. 540).

Today, the Shi'ites completely dominate Iran; their most prominent present leader is the Ayatollah Khoumeni.

The Sufis

In any strong, legalistic, religious system, worship can become mechanical and be exercised by rote, and God can become transcendent. Such an impersonal religion often motivates people to react. Such is the case with Islam, as the Sufis, the most well-known Islamic mystics, have arisen in response to orthodox Islam and to the often loose and secularist view of Islamic leadership during some of its early days under the *Ummayad* and *Abbasid* dynasties.

> Despite the claims of the Law, another aspect of Islam has been almost equally important for the rank and file of the faithful—this is Sūfism: mysticism, as it is usually translated.
> The Sūfīs are those Muslims who have most sought for direct personal experience of the Divine. While some of them have been legalists of the most fundamentalist stamp, their emphasis on direct religious experience has more often led the Sūfīs into tension with the legalists, and their attitude toward the Law has ranged from patronizing irony to outright hostility (John Alden Williams, *Islam*, New York: George Braziller, 1962, p. 136).

Describing the emergence of the Sufis, Noss states:

> Millions of Muslims had within themselves the natural human need to feel their religion as a personal and emotional experience. Islam had no priests, then or now, ordained and set apart for a life dedicated to the worship of God and the pursuit of holiness, and yet everyone knew that Muhammad had been a true man of God, wholly dedicated to his mission, who in the period before the revelations came had retired at times from the world to meditate in a cave. It was thus that he had become an instrument of God's truth.
> It was the popular yearning for the presence among them of unworldly men dedicated to God, asceticism, and holiness that encouraged the eventual emergence of Islamic mysticism (Noss, *op. cit.*, p. 535).

The Sūfīs exist today and probably are best known through their Dervish Orders (e.g., "the whirling Dervish").

There are many other sects and divergent groups among Islam, too numerous to detail here. One might mention that the Baha'i Faith, although significantly different from Islam today, had its roots in Islam.

Contemporary Islam

The rise of Israel as a prominent power has brought renewal to a once-anemic Islamic faith. Nationalism, coupled with the Islamic faith, has served as a raison d'etat for many in the Arab world as they stand against Israel, their enemy. At various times in the recent past, Arab alliances have been conceived, discussed and then have died. There was the United Arab Republic and later an alliance discussed between Egypt, Libya and Syria.

Grunebaum comments:

> The spectacular success of the Arab Muslims in establishing an empire by means of a small number of campaigns against the great powers of the day has never ceased to stimulate the wonderment and the admiration of the Muslim world and Western scholarship (G.E. von Grunebaum, *Modern Islam*, Berkeley: University of California Press, 1962, p. 1).

Neill amplifies:

> It is not surprising that the Islamic world has caught the fever of nationalism that is raging everywhere among the peoples of Asia and Africa. The special intensity and vigour of Islamic, and especially Arab, nationalism springs from a complex of causes—memories of past splendour, resentment over Muslim weakness and Christian strength, above all that obscure sense of malaise, the feeling that in some way history has gone awry, that somehow the purposes of God are not being fulfilled as the Muslim has a right to expect.
>
> The achievments of the post-war period have been considerable. Egyptian self-assertion has made the Middle East one of the chief problem areas in the world. Libya became independent after the war. Morocco and Tunis have since won their independence. In Algeria the story of detachment from France was long and painful. But here too, in 1962, the goal of total independence was attained. And so the story goes on (Stephen Neill, *Christian Faith and Other Faiths*, London: Oxford University Press, 1970, pp. 43, 44.

However, much of this discussion has been quelled with the Camp David accords which saw peace rise out of the Middle East between Israel and Egypt. Yet on another front, committed Islamic fundamentalists have drawn world attention to Iran, and also in Egypt where they allegedly assassinated President Anwar Sadat.

Nationalism is a strong sweeping movement in nations with majority Muslim populations.

In addition, secularism has increased as the practices of the West infiltrate nations. Some of these Western transfusions have been sudden—many Arab countries are accumulating new and previously unknown wealth in the form of petro-dollars. However, the secularism has also had a backlash effect as many of the Muslim countries, in an attempt to preserve their identity, are holding the line on imported Western customs.

Since Islam embraces not only religion but also culture, the future of the faith will be very much dependent on the state of the nations it thrives in today. With Arab nations prospering, this could turn out to be both a curse and a blessing to the Islamic faith. It may be good for its culture, but its faith could be seriously compromised.

> Islam is a rapidly spreading religion for several reasons. It is the state religion of Moslem countries and this gives it a strong cultural and political base. It has the appeal of a universal message because of its simple creed and tenets. Anyone can enter the *Ummah*, the community of faithful Muslims. There are no racial barriers and thus it spreads quickly among the black communities of Africa, and more recently, of America. Its five doctrines and five pillars can be easily communicated. In the West it is making appeals to the universal brotherhood of man, world peace, temperance, and the uplifting of women (Kenneth Boa, *Cults, World Religions, and You*, Wheaton, IL: Victor Books, 1977, p. 56).

The supremacy of Islam in the political and social (as well as religious) arenas is exemplified by the following quote from the Koran:

> Believers, have fear of Allah and stand with those who uphold the cause of truth. No cause have the people of Medina and the desert Arabs who dwell around them to forsake Allah's apostle or to jeopardize his life so as to safeguard their own; for they do not expose themselves to thirst or hunger or to any ordeal on account of the cause of Allah, nor do they stir a step which may provoke the unbelievers. Each loss they suffer at the enemy's hands shall be counted as a good deed in the sight of Allah: He will not deny the righteous of their recompense. Each sum they give, be it small or large, and each journey they undertake, shall be noted down, so that Allah may requite them for their noblest deeds.

It is not right that all the faithful should go to war at once. A band from each community should stay behind to instruct themselves in religion and admonish their men when they return, so that they may take heed.

Believers, make war on the infidels who dwell around you. Deal courteously with them. Know that Allah is with the righteous (N.J. Dawood, trans., *The Koran*, London: Penguin Books, 1956, p. 333).

The Teachings of Islam

Faith and Duty

The teachings of Islam are comprised both of faith *(imam)* and practice or duty *(din)*. Sir Norman Anderson explains:

> The faith and practice of Islam are governed by the two great branches of Muslim learning, theology and jurisprudence, to both of which some reference has already been made. Muslim theology (usually called "Tawhid" from its central doctrine of the Unity of the Godhead) defines all that a man should believe, while the law (Shari'a) prescribes everything that he should do. There is no priesthood and no sacraments. Except among the Sufis, Islam knows only exhortation and instruction from those who consider themselves, or are considered by others, adequately learned in theology or law.
>
> Unlike any other system in the world today the Shari'a embraces every detail of human life, from the prohibition of crime to the use of the toothpick, and from the organization of the State to the most sacred intimacies—or unsavoury aberrations—of family life. It is "the science of all things, human and divine," and divides all actions into what is obligatory or enjoined, what is praiseworthy or recommended, what is permitted or legally indifferent, what is disliked or deprecated, and what is forbidden (Anderson, *op. cit.*, p. 78).

These practices are mainly true of Sunni Islam, not of the divergent sects.

The Law: Shari'a

Islamic law *(Shari'a)* plays a central role in all Islamic culture. The structure of the law is that civil law rather than common law is generally practiced in England and the United States.

It must be emphasized that the *Shari'a* has been central to Islamic doctrine:

> The most important and fundamental religious concept of Islam is that of the *shari'a* which literally means a "path to the watering place" but in its religious application means the total way of life as explicitly or implicitly commanded by God. The word has been used in the Koran, which sometimes suggests that different religions have different shari'as but at other times that all religions have fundamentally one shari'a.
>
> The concept as formulated by Muslim religious teachers, includes both the doctrine or belief, and practice or the law. But historically the formulation and systemization of the law took place earlier than the crystallization of the formal theology. This, as shown below, had far-reaching consequences for the future development of Islam *(Encyclopedia Britannica*, s.v. "Islam," Chicago: William Benton Publishing Company, 1967, p. 664).

The controversy surrounding the law and theology and the fourfold division of the *Shari'a* led to the formulation and distinction of the Sunni and Shi'ite sects in Islam. Guillaume explains:

> In Chapter 5 a sketch of the sources of Muslim law and of the formation of the four main schools has been given. In certain countries certain matters have been taken out of the purview of the shari'a and now come within the scope of secular courts; but, broadly speaking, no change comparable with that which has taken and is taking place in Islamic countries today has been seen within Islam for a thousand years or more. Turkey, as everyone knows, has abolished the shari'a altogether. Officially it is a secular State, though actually the influence of Islam on the population, especially in Asia, is very considerable, and shows signs of becoming stronger under the new democratic government.
>
> In a series of articles in *The Moslem World* and elsewhere my colleague, Mr. J.N.D. Anderson, has shown how in the Arab countries, too, the shari'a is undergoing revision. Egypt, the Sudan, Syria, Lebanon, Jordan, and Iraq are all on the move. The changes which are being made illustrate how a definite attempt to relate the shari'a to the conditions of modern life and to a more liberal view of human relations is being realized in positive legislation (Guillaume, *op. cit.,* pp. 166, 167).

He then comments on one of the differences of the Shi'ites and the Sunnis:

In theory, the Shi'ite conception of the supreme authority in law is utterly different from that of the Sunnis, though in practice the difference does not amount to very much. They reject the four schools and the doctrine of *ijmā* because their Hidden Imam has the sole right of determining what the believer shall do and believe. Therefore their duly accredited doctors can still exercise the power of *ijtihād* or personal opinion. This power the Sunnis lost a thousand years ago or more (Guillaume, *op. cit.*, p. 103).

Qur'an

The basis for Islamic doctrine is found in the Qur'an (Koran). Boa describes the central place of the Qur'an in the Islamic faith as well as the supplementary works:

> The Koran is the authoritative scripture of Islam. About four-fifths the length of the New Testament, it is divided into 114 surahs (chapters). Parts were written by Mohammed, and the rest, based on his oral teaching, was written from memory by his disciples after Mohammed's death.
>
> Over the years a number of additional sayings of Mohammed and his early disciples were compiled. These comprise the *Hadith* ("tradition"), the sayings of which are called *sunna* ("custom"). The Hadith supplements the Koran much as the Talmud supplements the Law in Judaism (Kenneth Boa, *op. cit.*, p. 52).

The Qur'an is the Word of God in Islam, the holy scriptures. As the authoritative scripture, it is the main guide for all matters of faith and practice. The Qur'an was revealed to Muhammad as the Word of God for mankind.

Other revelations include the *Torat* (of Moses), the *Suhuf* (books of the prophets), *Zabur* (psalms of David), *Injil* (gospel of Jesus). The Qur'an supercedes all other revelations and is the only one of which we still have the original text. All of the others have been corrupted, almost beyond recognition.

Islam, for example, would not consider our New Testament to be the Injil (gospel of Jesus). It is not the words of Jesus, it is others' words *about* Jesus. His original words have been corrupted and many have been lost. Only the Qur'an is infallible. Muhammad and the Qur'an are that which Islam is to follow.

Neill comments:

It is well known that at many points the Qur'an does not
agree with the Jewish and Christian Scriptures. Therefore,
from the Muslim point of view, it follows of necessity that
these Scriptures must have been corrupted. Historical
evidence makes no impression on the crushing force of the
syllogism. So it is, and it can be no other way. The Muslim
controversialist feels no need to study evidence in detail. The
only valid picture of Jesus Christ is that which is to be found
in the pages of the Qur'an (Stephen Neill, *op. cit.*, p. 64).

The Qur'an is comprised of 114 *surahs*, or chapters, all
attributed to Muhammad. The surahs are arranged in the
Qur'an by length — the longer in front, the shorter in back.

For the Muslims, the Koran *(q.v.)* is the Word of God, con-
firming and consummating earlier revealed books and
thereby replacing them; its instrument or agent of revelation
is the Prophet Mohammed, the last and most perfect of a
series of messengers of God to mankind — from Adam through
Abraham to Moses and Jesus, the Christian claims for whose
divinity are strongly rejected. Indeed there is no people to
whom a prophet has not come. Although Mohammed is only
a human creature of God, he has nevertheless an unequaled
importance in the Koran itself which sets him only next to
God as deserving of moral and legal obedience. Hence, his
sayings and deeds (Sunna) served as a second basis, besides
the Koran, of the belief and practice of Islam.

The Koran (which, for the Muslim, is the miracle par
excellence of Mohammed, unsurpassable in form as well as in
content) is a forceful document basically expressing an *élan*
of religious and social justice. The early chapters (suras) of
the Koran, reflecting Mohammed's grim struggle against the
Meccans, are characterized by grave warnings of the im-
minent judgment, while the later suras, of the Medina
period, are chiefly directed to regulating the internal and
external affairs of the young Muslim community-state,
besides narrating the stories of the earlier prophets.

The koranic theology is rigorously monotheistic: God is
absolutely unique — "there is nothing like him" —
omnipotent, omniscient, merciful. Men are exhorted to obey
his will *(i.e., to be Muslim)* as is necessarily done by all
inorganic objects. Special responsibility is laid on man who
willingly, although with his characteristically foolish pride,
accepted "the trust," refused by all creation. Besides human
beings and angels, the Koran speaks of the jinn, both good and
evil, to whom sometimes the devil is represented as
belonging (*Encyclopedia Britannica, op. cit.*, p. 663).

In modern times, the Qur'an has faced many of the same dilemmas as the Bible. A major issue is the inspiration of the Qur'an. Islamic scholars do not agree as a whole on how the Qur'an came to be true or how much is true, although conservative Islamic scholars accept it *all* as literally true. John Alden Williams comments:

> The Qur'an, then, is the Word of God, for Muslims. While controversies have raged among them as to the sense in which this is true—whether it is the created or uncreated Word, whether it is true of every Arabic letter or only of the message as a whole, that it *is true* has never been questioned by them (John Alden Williams, *op. cit.*, p. 15).

The Qur'an was revealed and written in the Arabic language. Because of this, and the fact it was revealed by God, Muslims deplore translations of the Qur'an into other languages. There is, then, no *authoritative* translation for the Qur'an. Anyone familiar with the reading of translations of any work would be sympathetic to this demand. However, as rich as Arabic is, the translations still provide a close original which can and must be evaluated for its validity, not simply its reliability.

The Qur'an came into written form shortly after Muhammad's death.

> All the sûrahs of the Koran had been recorded in writing before the Prophet's death, and many Muslims had committed the whole Koran to memory. But the written sûrahs were dispersed among the people; and when, in a battle which took place during the Caliphate of Abû Bakr—that is to say, within two years of the Prophet's death—a large number of those who knew the whole Koran by heart were killed, a collection of the whole Koran was made and put in writing. In the Caliphate of Othmân, all existing copies of sûrahs were called in, and an authoritative version, based on Abû Bakr's collection and the testimony of those who had the whole Koran by heart, was compiled exactly in the present form and order, which is regarded as traditional and as the arrangement of the Prophet himself, the Caliph Othmân and his helpers being Comrades of the Prophet and the most devout students of the Revelation. The Koran has thus been very carefully preserved (Mohammed Marmaduke Pickthall, trans., *The Meaning of the Glorious Koran*, New York: Mentor Books, n.d., p. xxviii).

On the origin of the Qur'an, Guillaume comments:

From the books of tradition we learn that the prophet was subject to ecstatic seizures. He is reported to have said that when inspiration came to him he felt as it were the painful sounding of a bell. Even in cold weather his forehead was bathed in sweat. On one occasion he called to his wife to wrap him in a veil. At other times visions came to him in sleep. Religious ecstasy is a world-wide phenomenon in one stage of human society, and in its early stages Muhammad's verses were couched in the Semitic form of mantic oracular utterance. The veiling of the head and the use of rhymed prose were marks of the Arabian soothsayer, while the feeling of physical violence and compulsion, and the outward appearance of "possession" which seemed to the onlookers to indicates madness or demonic possession were sometimes recorded by, or observed in, the Hebrew prophets.

The Qur'an as we have it now is a record of what Muhammad said while in the state or states just mentioned. It is beyond doubt that his hearers recognized the symptoms of revelation, otherwise his *obiter dicta* which the literature of tradition purports to record would be included in the Qur'an (Guillaume, *op. cit.*, p. 56).

Five Articles of Faith

The five articles of faith are the main doctrines of Islam. All Muslims are expected to believe these tenets.

1. *God.* There is only one true God and his name is Allah. Allah is all-knowing, all-powerful and the sovereign judge. Yet Allah is not a personal God, for he is so far above man in every way that he is not personally knowable. Noss states:

In the famous Muslim creedal formula the first part reads: *lā ilāha illa Allāh*, "(There is) no god but God." This is the most important article in Muslim theology. No statement about God seemed to Muhammad more fundamental than the declaration that God is one, and no sin seemed to him so unpardonable as associating another being with God on terms of equality. God stands alone and supreme. He existed before any other being or thing, is self-subsistent, omniscient, omnipotent ("all-seeing, all-hearing, all-willing"). He is the creator, and in the awful day of judgment he is the sole arbiter who shall save the believer out of the dissolution of the world and place him in paradise (Noss, *op. cit.*, p. 517).

This doctrine, which makes God different from His creatures, is strong in Islam. Allah is so different that it makes it (1) difficult to really know very much about him, and (2) unlikely that he is affected by his creatures' attitudes or actions. Although Allah is said to be loving, this aspect of his nature is almost ignored, and his supreme attribute of justice is thought to overrule love (Anderson, *op. cit.*, p. 79).

The emphasis of the God of Islam is on judgment, not grace; on power, not mercy. He is the source of both good and evil and his will is supreme.

2. *Angels.* The existence of angels is fundamental to Islamic teaching. Gabriel, the leading angel, appeared to Muhammad and was instrumental in delivering the revelations in the Qur'an to Muhammad. Al Shaytan is the devil and most likely a fallen angel or jinn. Jinn are those creatures between angels and men which can be either good or evil.

Angels do not perform any bodily functions (sexual, eating, etc.) as they are created of light. All angels have different purposes, such as Gabriel, or Jibril, who is the messenger of inspiration. Each man or woman also has two recording angels — one who records his good deeds, the other, his bad deeds.

3. *Scripture.* There are four inspired books in the Islamic faith. They are the *Torah* of Moses, the Psalms *(Zabin)* of David, the Gospel of Jesus Christ *(Injil)* and the *Qur'an.* Muslims believe the former three books have been corrupted by Jews and Christians. Also, since the Qur'an is god's most recent and final word to man, it supercedes all the other works.

4. *Prophets.* In Islam God has spoken through numerous prophets down through the centuries. The six greatest are: Adam, Noah, Abraham, Moses, Jesus and Muhammad. Muhammad is the last and greatest of all Allah's messengers.

5. *Last Days.* The last day will be a time of resurrection and judgment. Those who follow and obey Allah and Muhammad will go to Islamic heaven, called Paradise, a place of pleasure. Those who oppose them will be tormented in hell.

The last day (the resurrection and the judgment) figures prominently in Muslim thought. The day and hour is a secret to all, but there are to be twenty-five signs of its approach. All men will then be raised; the books kept by the recording angels will be opened; and God as judge will weigh each man's deeds in the balances. Some will be admitted to Paradise, where they will recline on soft couches quaffing cups of wine handed them by the Huris, or maidens of Paradise, of whom each man may marry as many as he pleases; others will be consigned to the torments of Hell. Almost all, it would seem, will have to enter the fire temporarily, but no true Muslim will remain there forever (Anderson, *op. cit.* p. 81).

Finally there is a sixth article of faith which is considered by many to belong to the five doctrines. Whether this is one of the articles or not, it is a central teaching of Islam — the belief in God's decrees or Kismet, the doctrine of fate. This is a very rigid view of predestination that states all good or evil proceeds from divine will.

This strong fatalism has played a central role in Muslim culture. "To this the lethargy and lack of progress which, until recently at least, has for centuries characterized Muslim countries, can be partially attributed" (Anderson, *op. cit.*, p. 82). From this concept comes the most common Islamic phrase, roughly translated, "It is Allah's will."

Five Pillars of Faith

Besides the five major beliefs or doctrines in Islam, there are also "five pillars of faith." These are observances in Islam which are foundational practices or duties every Muslim must observe. The five are: The Creed, Prayers, Almsgiving, Fasting and the Pilgrimage to Mecca.

1. *The Creed. (Kalima).* "There is no God but Allah, and Muhammad is the Prophet of Allah," is the bedrock of Muslim belief. One must state this aloud publicly in order to become a Muslim. It is repeated constantly by the faithful.

2. *Prayer (Salat).* Prayer as ritual is central to a devout Muslim. Boa comments:

The practice of prayer *(salat)* five times a day (upon rising, at noon, in midafternoon, after sunset, and before retiring). The worshipper must recite the prescribed prayers (the first surah and other selections from the Koran) in Arabic while facing the Ka'aba in Mecca. The Hadith (book of tradition) has turned these prayers into a mechanical procedure of standing, kneeling, hands and face on the ground, and so forth. The call to prayer is sounded by the *muezzin* (a Muslim crier) from a tower called a *minaret* which is part of the *mosque* (the place of public worship) (Boa, *op. cit.*, p. 53).

3. *Almsgiving (Zakat)*. Muhammad, himself an orphan, had a strong desire to help the needy. The alms originally were voluntary, but all Muslims are legally required to give one-fortieth of their income for the destitute. There are other rules and regulations for produce, cattle, etc. Freewill offerings also can be exercised.

Since those to whom alms are given are helping the giver to salvation, they feel no sense of debt to the giver. On the contrary, it is the giver's responsibility and duty to give and he should consider himself lucky he has someone to give to.

4. *Fasting (Ramadan)*. Faithful Muslims fast from sunup to sundown each day during this holy month. The fast develops self-control, devotion to God and identity with the destitute. No food or drink may be consumed during the daylight hours; no smoking or sexual pleasures may be enjoyed, either. Many Muslims eat two meals a day during Ramadan, one before sunrise and one shortly after sunset.

5. *The Pilgrimage (Hajj)*. The pilgrimage is expected of all Muslims at least once in their lifetimes. It can be extremely arduous on the old or infirm, so in their cases they may send someone in their places. The trip is an essential part in Muslims' gaining salvation. It involves a set of ceremonies and rituals, many of which center around the Ka'aba shrine, to which the pilgrimage is directed. Of the Ka'aba, Muhammad M. Pickthall comments in *The Meaning of the Glorious Koran*:

> The Meccans claimed descent from Abraham through Ishmael, and tradition stated that their temple, the Ka'aba, had been built by Abraham for the worship of the One God. It was still called the House of Allah, but the chief objects of worship there were a number of idols which were called daughters of Allah and intercessors (Pickthall, *op. cit.*, p. ix).

The idols were destroyed by Muhammad on his return to Mecca in power following the *Hijira* (exile).

> When the pilgrim is about six miles from the holy city, he enters upon the state of *ihram:* he casts off, after prayers, his ordinary clothes and puts on two seamless garments; he walks almost barefooted and neither shaves, cuts his hair nor cuts his nails. The principle activity consists of a visit to the Sacred mosque *(al-Masjid al-Haram)*; the kissing of the Black Stone *(al-Hajar al-Aswad)*; seven circumambulations of the Ka'aba three times running and four times slowly; the visit to the sacred stone called Maqam Ibrahim; the ascent of and running between Mt. Safa and Mt. Marwa seven times; the visit to Mt. Arafat; the hearing of a sermon there and spending the night at Muzdalifa; the throwing of stones at the three pillars at Mina and offering sacrifice on the last day of Ihram, which is the '*id* of sacrifice *('Id al-Adha)* (*Encyclopedia Britannica, op. cit.*, p. 664).

This Muslim pilgrimage serves to heighten and solidify Islamic faith.

There is a sixth religious duty associated with the five pillars. This is *Jihad*, the Holy War. This duty requires that when the situation warrants, men are required to go to war to spread Islam or defend it against infidels. One who dies in a *Jihad* is guaranteed eternal life in Paradise (heaven).

Cultural Expression

Islam, like Judaism, is both a religion and a cultural identity which cannot be separated from the people. In many countries the Islamic faith, though not strictly practiced, is woven into the web of society at every facet.

The Cambridge History of Islam comments on this phenomenon:

> Islam is a religion. It is also, inseparably from this, a community, a civilization and a culture. It is true that many of the countries through which the Qur'anic faith spread already possessed ancient and important cultures. Islam absorbed these cultures, and assimilated itself to them in various ways, to a far greater extent than it attempted to supplant them. But in doing this, it provided them with attributes in common, with a common attitude toward God, to men and to the world, and thus ensured, through the

diversities of language, of history and of race, the complex unity of the *dār al-Islām*, the "house" or "world" of Islam.

The history of the Muslim peoples and countries is thus a unique example of a culture with a religious foundation, uniting the spiritual and the temporal, sometimes existing side by side with "secular" cultures, but most often absorbing them by becoming very closely interlinked with them (P. M. Holt, *op. cit.*, Vol. I, p. 569).

Language and the Arts

To doctrine which serves as both a religious and social foundation, the Arabic language can be added as another unifying factor which helps weld Islamic peoples together.

There is an abundance of Arabic poetry and prose in which the Islamic faith is placed in high regard. Muslim art and architecture also have a highly developed style. Many of the mosques and minarets are tremendous works of art decorated with intricate arabesque ornamentation.

The Family

The family is very important in the social economy of Islam. Marriage is required for every Muslim, even the ascetics. Muhammed commanded men to marry and propagate the race. Men may not have more than four wives, yet many cohabit with as many concubines as they choose.

Although the act of marriage is important, the sanctity of the union is not as highly regarded. A Muslim may divorce his wife at any time and for any reason. On the whole, women in Islamic culture do not enjoy the status or the privileges of the men and are very dependent on their husbands. While this sounds cruel and sexist to Westerners, it was a humane innovation in Muhammad's time. Islamic law requires what was then unheard of: each wife must be treated equally.

Other practices include the veiling of women, circumcision, abstention from alcohol, gambling and certain foods. Many of the above, such as alcohol and gambling, are seen as vices of the West.

Islam and Christianity

Many of the Muslim beliefs come from the Bible. The

historical foundation for the Qur'an comes from the Old Testament. Yet even though there has been influence and there are similarities, the differences in the beliefs of the two faiths are striking.

God

Islam teaches the unity of God's essence and personality, explicitly excluding the Trinity as taught in the Bible.

This emphasis on the unity of God comes across in other ways. Islam has God divorced from His creation, so unified to Himself that He cannot be associated with creation. His transcendence is so great that He acts impersonally.

Because of their doctrine of predestination and the fact that both evil and good came from Allah, it makes their God very capricious. Whatever Allah chooses becomes right; this makes any true standard of righteousness or ethics hard to discern if not impossible to establish.

This is unlike the God of the Bible who is righteous. The very word righteous means, "a standard."

The Muslim finds it difficult to divorce the concept of father from the physical realm. To them it is blasphemous to call Allah or God your father. To do so is the same as saying that your mother and Allah and sexual intercourse to produce you!

In addition, while calling God "Father" is to evoke thoughts of love, compassion, tenderness and protectiveness to Christians, it is not so to the Muslim mind. To him, a father is strict, shows no emotion, never expresses love, and is bound to his family by duty and for what his family can provide for him, not by devotion.

Allah is also very deficient in such attributes as love, holiness and grace. Grace, of course, is rooted in the character of God (Ephesians 2).

The Bible

As mentioned before, the Muslim holy books include the sayings of Moses, the prophets, David, Jesus and Muhammad. However, all of the previous sayings have been lost or corrupted. Only the Qur'an, the words of Muhammad, have been preserved free of error. They also supercede the previous revelations. Remember, the holy books mentioned in Islam are *not* exactly like our biblical Scriptures.

One would presuppose that since the teachings of Christianity and Islam are clearly different, it would follow that the practical and social consequences of the doctrine would also be vastly different. This is precisely the case. As Guillaume mentions, this is nowhere better illustrated than in the status of women:

> The Qur'an has more to say on the position of women than on any other social question. The guiding note is sounded in the words, "Women are your tillage," and the word for marriage is that used for the sexual act. The primary object of marriage is the propagation of children, and partly for this a man is allowed four wives at a time and an unlimited number of concubines. However, it is laid down that wives are to be treated with kindness and strict impartiality; if a man cannot treat all alike he should keep to one.
>
> The husband pays the woman a dowry at the time of marriage, and the money or property so alloted remains her own. The husband may divorce his wife at any time, but he cannot take her back until she has remarried and been divorced by a second husband. A woman cannot sue for divorce on any grounds, and her husband may beat her. In this matter of the status of women lies the greatest difference between the Muslim and the Christian world.
>
> Since Muslim propagandists in this country persistently deny that women are inferior to men in Islam it is worthwhile to set out the facts. Sura 4:31 says: "Men have authority over women because God has made the one superior to the other and because they spend their wealth [to maintain them]. So good women are obedient, guarding the unseen [parts] because God has guarded [them]. As for those from whom you fear disobedience admonish them and banish them to beds apart and beat them; then if they obey you seek not occasion against them (Guillaume, *op. cit.*, pp. 71, 72).

Christ

In Islam the person and work of Jesus Christ are not seen in the same way as in Christianity. For the Christian the resurrection of Jesus Christ as the incarnate Son of God is the vital cornerstone of faith, yet the Muslim does not hold to either of these truths — that Christ is the Son of God or that he rose from dead. In fact, Muslims do not even believe Jesus was crucified; rather, many believe Judas was crucified in His place. Some, however, believe it was Christ on the cross but that He did not die.

Islam does believe Jesus was a sinless prophet although not as great as Muhammad. While Surah 3:45-47 in the Qur'an speaks of the virgin birth of Christ, it is not the same biblical virgin birth. Jesus is certainly *not* the only begotten Son of God, and an angel—rather than the Holy Spirit—was the agency of God's power in the conception. However, the idea that Allah had a son is repugnant to them. Surah 4:171 states, "Jesus...was only a messenger of Allah...Far is it removed from His transcendent majesty that He should have a son."

John states concerning Christ, "And the Word became flesh, and dwelt among us, and we beheld His glory, glory as of the only begotten from the Father, full of grace and truth...And I have seen, and have borne witness that this is the Son of God" (John 1:14, 34).

Christ's claim for His own deity and Sonship are unequivocal. In John 10:30 He claims equality with the Father when He states, "I and the Father are one." For not only is the Sonship of Christ important per se, but the deity of Christ is also an important point of difference between Christianity and Islam since Islam denies the doctrine of the Trinity.

Of the crucifixion, the Qur'an states in Surah 4:157, "They slew him not nor crucified, but it appeared so unto them..." Most Muslims believe Judas was put in the place of Christ, and Christ went to heaven. The Bible teaches that Christ went to the cross to pay the penalty for man's sins, died, and was raised from the dead, appeared to the disciples and *then* ascended to heaven.

Paul recounts the events this way: "For I delivered to you as of first importance what I also received, that Christ died for our sins according to the Scriptures, and that He was buried, and that He was raised on the third day according to the Scriptures, and that He appeared to Cephas and then to the twelve. After that He appeared to more than five hundred" (2 Corinthians 15:3-6, NASB).

Of the importance of the resurrection, Paul states, "And if Christ has not been raised, your faith is worthless; you are still in your sins" (2 Corinthians 15:17, NASB).

Max Kershaw, in *"How to Share the Good News with Your Muslim Friend,"* states:

In this regard, the Muslim view of Jesus is significant. The Qur'an presents Jesus as one of the great prophets. He is called the Messiah. He is declared to have been born of the virgin Mary. He lived a sinless life (Surah 19:19). He accomplished many wonderful miracles, such as the giving of sight to the blind, healing of lepers and the raising of the dead (3:49). He is going to return to the earth again to establish Islam throughout the earth. He is called "the Word of God" (3:45) and "the Spirit from God" (4:171). Thus, Muslims have a high view of Jesus.

But they are adamant in declaring that Jesus is not the **Son of God** and **Savior.** In fact, they believe that equating anyone with God is blasphemy, the unforgiveable sin. More than this, they do not believe that he was crucified. Instead, God took him to heaven without dying, and someone else died in his place. One particular passage in the Qur'an (4:156-158) seems to say this, but it is not clear. In fact, other Qur'anic passages speak of the death of Jesus (19:33) (Max R. Kershaw, *How to Share the Good News with Your Muslim Friend,* Colorado Springs: International Students, Inc., 1978, p.).

Boa comments:

Unlike the God of the Bible, Allah has done nothing for man that cost him anything. Islam makes no real provision for sin. One's salvation is never certain since it is based on a works system and on complete surrender ("Islam") to the will of Allah. This religion rejects the biblical teaching of the crucifixion and resurrection of Jesus, though it concedes that He was a sinless prophet. Mohammed did not rise from the dead, and there is no basis for a resurrection in Islam (Boa, *op. cit.,* p. 55).

Neill states with respect to Islam and the person of Christ:

It is perfectly true that the central concern of Jesus was with the kingdom of God. But everything depends on the meaning that is put into the word "God." Here is perhaps the very heart of our differences. Islam conceives the possible relationship of man to God in one way, and the Gospel in another.

While God was the exclusive source of the revelation to Muhammad, God himself is not the content of the revelation. Revelation in Islamic theology does not mean God disclosing himself. It is revelation *from* God, not revelation *of* God. God is remote. He is inscrutable and utterly inaccessible to human knowledge...Even though we are his creatures whose every breath is dependent upon him, it is not in inter-personal relationship with him that we receive guidance from him.

At this central point the teaching of Jesus diverges from what the Muslim believes to be the essential prophetic witness. His God is a God who cares for his creatures, who is prepared to enter into fellowship with them, and is concerned that they should love him in response to his love. Under the law man was in the position of a slave; now under the Gospel he is called to freedom, to the freedom of grown-up sons in their Father's house. The Qur'an never uses the word "Father" of God. Jesus taught his disciples to address him as "Our Father." The whole of the Gospel is summed up in these two words.

If the possibility is admitted that God might be such as Jesus declared him to be, the incarntion presents itself no longer as a blasphemous and irrational impossibility, but as something that appears even appropriate, in the light of this new perception of what the fatherhood of God might be.

The death of Christ at the hands of the Jews is rejected by Muslims on *a priori* grounds, which are absolutely convincing if the major premise is admitted. It is impossible that God should so desert a prophet in the fulfillment of his mission. It would be contrary to His justice to permit the suffering of an innocent on behalf of others. It would be contrary to His omnipotence not to be able to rescue a prophet in danger. Therefore Jesus cannot have been left helpless in the hands of his enemies (Neill, *op. cit.,* pp. 66, 67).

Sin and Salvation

The previous differences between Islam and Christianity find fruit in the teachings of salvation. Neill comments:

At the heart of the Muslim-Christian disagreement, we shall find a deep difference in the understanding of the nature of sin. It is not true to say that the Muslim has no sense of sin or of the need for forgiveness. He has both. But sin reveals its deadly nature only when it is seen in its effects on personal relationships; and such an understanding of it is almost necessarily excluded, as we have seen, by the Muslim's concept of the possible relationship between the believer and his God. The believer may sin against the law and the majesty of God, and if he does so he deserves to be punished. The idea that man by his sin might break the heart of God is not yet within the spectrum of the Muslim understanding of reality (Neill, *op. cit.*, pp. 68, 69).

The Muslim operates under a legalistic system and must earn his salvation. He holds to the *Articles of Faith* and follows the *Pillars of Faith*. For the Muslim, sin is lack of obedience to Allah. Thus, man is sinful by act only, not by nature.

The Bible teaches that man is sinful by nature. Paul writes to the Romans, "For all have sinned and fall short of the glory of God" (Romans 3:23, NASB).

These are historical roots which tie Islam to Christianity, yet this is where the similarity ends. Islam rejects the key doctrines of the Christian faith—the Trinity, the deity of Christ, Christ's crucifixion and resurrection, and the sin of man and his salvation by grace alone through faith in Christ.

They also reject the Bible as the only authoritative book on which to base all matters of doctrine, faith and practice. When Islam rejects the truth of the written Word of God, they are left not only different from Christianity, but opposite from Christianity on all counts. Islam was founded by a dead prophet; Christianity was founded by the risen Savior.

Conclusion

Islam is one of the driving forces among world religions today, its growth closely tied to nationalism. But growth does not mean truth.

The God of Islam is a very capricious one, too far removed from people to be personally involved or concerned. Not only is he impersonal, but he also emphasized judgment to the exclusion of love, and he motivates people by fear rather than by grace.

Muhammad, the founder, has based his teaching on inaccurate and untrue interpretations of the Bible. There is no historical evidence to support Muhammad's contentions that either the Jewish or Christian scriptures have been corrupted. In addition, his teaching in the Qur'an is based on revelations which he initially believed were demonic in origin.

Islam is an aggressive and impressive world religion. It appeals to those who welcome a religious world view which permeates every facet of life. However, it is ultimately unfulfilling. The Islamic God of strict judgment, Allah, cannot offer the mercy, love, and ultimate sacrifice on mankind's behalf that the Christian God, incarnate in Jesus Christ, offers to each man even today.

Islamic Terms

ABU BAKR—(Reign: 632-634 A.D.) The first Moslem caliph, according to Sunni Muslims. The Shi'ite Muslims reject this and instead consider the fourth caliph, 'Alī, as the first true successor to Mohammad.

ALLAH—The Supreme Being. The name of God, derived from the Arabic *Al-Ilāh*.

CALIPH—the title given to office of the spiritual and political leadership which took over after Mohammad's death.

FATIMA—The daughter of Mohammad and his first wife; and the wife of 'Ali, the fourth Caliph.

HADITH—The sacred sayings of Mohammad, handed down by oral tradition, for generations after Mohammad's death until finally transcribed.

HAJJ—A pilgrimage to Mecca. One of the five pillars of the Islamic faith.

HEGIRA—Mohammad's flight from Mecca to present day Medina in 622 A.D.

IMAM—A Moslem who is considered by Sunnis to be an authority in Islamic law and theology or the man who leads the prayers. Also refers to each of the founders of the four principal sects of Islam. The Shi'ites accept 12 great Imams.

ISLAM—Literally, "submission to the will of Allah."

KA'ABA—A small stone building located in the court of the great mosque at Mecca containing the black stone (a meteorite) supposedly given to Abraham by Gabriel.

KORAN (QUR'AN)—Said to be the final and complete inspired word of God transmitted to the prophet Mohammad by the angel Gabriel.

MAHDI—"The guided one." A leader who will cause righteousness to fill the earth. The Sunnites are still awaiting his initial appearance while the Shi'ites hold that the last Imam, who disappeared in 874 A.D. will someday reappear as the Mahdi.

MECCA—The birthplace of Mohammad. This city, located in Saudi Arabia, is considered the most holy city by the Moslems.

MEDINA—A holy city of Islam named for Mohammad. It was previously named Yathrib. It is the city to which Mohammad fled in 622 A.D.

MOHAMMAD—The prophet and founder of Islam. Born around 570 A.D., died 632 A.D.

MOSLEM (MUSLIM)—A follower of Mohammad. Literally, "one who submits."

MOSQUE—An Islamic place of worship.

MUEZZIN—A Moslem crier who announces the hour of prayer.

MULLA—A teacher of Islamic laws and doctrines.

OMAR—According to the Sunnites, the second Moslem caliph and principal advisor to the first caliph, Abu Bakr.

PURDAY—A veil or covering used by Moslem women to ensure them privacy against public observation, and to indicate their submission.

RAMADAN—The ninth month of the Moslem year, when Mohammad received the Qur'an from heaven, and now devoted to fasting.

SALAT—The Moslem daily prayer ritual. One of the five pillars of Islamic faith.

SHI'ITES—A Moslem sect which rejects the first three caliphs, insisting that Mohammad's son-in-law 'Ali was Mohammad's rightful initial successor.

SUFIS—Iranian (Persian) philosophical mystics who have largely adapted and reinterpreted Islam for themselves.

SUNNITES—The largest Moslem sect which acknowledges the first four caliphs as Mohammad's rightful successors.

SURAHS—What the chapters of the Qur'an are called.

Islam Bibliography

Anderson, Sir Norman, *The World's Religions*, Grand Rapids, MI: William B. Eerdmans Publishing Company, 1976.

Boa, Kenneth, *Cults, World Religions, and You*, Wheaton, IL: Victor Books, 1977.

Davood, N. J., trans., *The Koran*, London: Penguin Books, 1956.

Holt, P. M., and Lambton, and Lewis, eds., *The Cambridge History of Islam*, London: Cambridge University Press, 1970.

Encyclopedia Britannica, s.v. "Islam," Chicago: William Benton Publisher, 1967.

Grunebaum, G. E. von, *Modern Islam*, Berkeley: University of California Press, 1962.

Guillaume, Alfred, *Islam*, London: Penguin Books, 1954.

Kershaw, Max R., *How to Share the Good News with Your Muslim Friend*, Colorado Springs: International Students Inc., 1978.

Neill, Stephen, *Christian Faith and Other Faiths*, London: Oxford University Press, 1970.

Noss, John B., *Man's Religions*, New York: MacMillan Publishing Company Inc., 1974.

Payne, Robert, *The Holy Sword*, New York: Collier Books, 1962.

Pickthall, Mohammed Marmaduke, trans., *The Meaning of the Glorious Koran*, New York: Mentor Books, n.d.

Williams, John Alden, *Islam*, New York: George Braziller, 1962.

Sikhism

Sikhism is a religion all but unknown to western civilization. Its adherents are to be found for the most part in the Punjab province of India. A fairly recent religion, Sikhism is an attempt to harmonize two of the world's greater religions, Hinduism and Islam. Sikhism is the third major branch of Hinduism and was founded by a man named Nanak. It also owes much to Islam.

History of Sikhism

Nanak: the Founder

Nanak was born in the Indian village of Talwandi, some 30 miles southwest of Lahore, capital of Punjab. The date of his birth is given as 1469 A.D. His parents were common people who embraced the Hindu religion. There are folk stories of Nanak's youth which depict him charging a Hindu teacher to know the true name of God.

At an early age, Nanak supposedly gave religious instruction to certain Brahman priests concerning the material sacrament. Whether these stories are true or not, his life was devoted more to meditation and religion than to work. The occupations chosen for him by his parents were not satisfying and caused him to be somewhat of a black sheep within his family. He eventually took a government position which was offered him by his brother-in-law in another town. However, Nanak remained unhappy and continued his constant search for religious truth.

At the age of 33 he was said to have received his divine call.

> One day after bathing, Nanak disappeared into the forest and was taken in a vision to God's presence. He was offered a cup of nectar, which he gratefully accepted. God said to him: "I am with thee. I have made thee happy, and also those who shall take thy name. Go, and repeat Mine, and cause others to do likewise. Abide uncontaminated by the world. Practice the repetition of my Name, charity, ablutions, worship, and meditation... My Name is God, the primal Brahma. And thou are the divine Guru" (M. A. McAuliffe, *Sikh Religion: Its Gurus, Sacred Writings, and Authors*, London: Oxford University Press, 1909, pp. 33-35).

Three days later Nanak returned from the forest and after remaining silent for one day, he pronounced, "There is no Hindu and no Musalman" (*Ibid.*, p. 37). In India, Muslims are known as "Musalmans."

Nanak, along with his minstrel friend Mardana, proceeded to proclaim his new-found message with relatively little success until they returned to Punjab. Disciples were now gathered around him and the newly found faith continued to grow throughout his life. Around age 70 Nanak died, but not without first appointing a successor to continue his mission. The choice was his trusted disciple Angad. According to tradition, even in death, Nanak appeased both Hindu and Muslim.

> The Musalmans, who had received God's name from the Guru, said they would bury him after his death. His Hindu followers, on the contrary, said they would cremate him. When the Guru was invited to decide the discussion, he said: "Let the Hindus place flowers on my right, and the Musalmans on my left. They whose flowers are found fresh in the morning, may have the disposal of my body." Guru Nanak then ordered the crowd to sing: "O my friends, pray for me that I may meet my Lord." The Guru drew a sheet over him, made obeisance to God, and blended his light with Guru Angad's [his successor].... When the sheet was removed the next morning, there was nothing found beneath it. The flowers on both sides were in bloom. All the Sikhs reverently saluted the spot on which the Guru had lain...at Kartepur in the Punjab. The Sikhs erected a shrine, and the Muhammadans a tomb in his honour on the margin of the Ravi. Both have since been washed away by the river (*Ibid.*, pp. 190, 191).

Development of Sikhism

Prior to his death, Nanak appointed a ropemaker named Lahina as his successor. It was Lahina who thereafter changed his name to Angad (bodyguard), and who introduced the doctrine of Nanak's equality with God. A series of different gurus followed Angad, one of whom was Guru Arjan, who compiled the *Granth Sahib* during his leadership.

After the tenth guru in the line of succession died in 1708, the loyalty of the Sikhs was transferred from the personal authority of the guru to the sacred book, the *Granth Sahib*, and so it remains today.

The Teachings of Sikhism

The teachings of Sikhism are a syncretism of the doctrines of Islam and Hinduism. Rather than borrowing from the Hindu and Islamic scriptures, the Sikhs wrote their own scripture based upon their interpretation of certain ideas taught in Hinduism and Islam. Sikhism actually rejects some of the teachings of Hinduism and Islam. The result is an interesting combination of both Hindu and Moslem theology.

Scripture

The sacred scriptures of Sikhism are known as the *Granth Sahib* or "Lord's Book." This work was composed by several dozen authors, some living prior to Nanak and having only a distant relationship to Sikhism. It contains a collection of poems of various lengths and totals some 29,480 rhymed verses. The contents center on extolling the name of God and exhortations on daily living.

A unique feature of this work is the number of languages utilized in its composition. The *Granth Sahib* is written in six different languages and several dialects. It is therefore nearly impossible for even the learned Sikh to study these scriptures in their entirety, much less so for the unlearned.

Undoubtedly, there are only a handful of people in the entire world capable of reading the volume in its totality. There has never been any extensive system of scriptural study made by the Sikhs. The average Sikh devotee knows very little about the *Granth Sahib*, and it is for this reason non-essential to Sikh religious training. Although most

Sikhs do not know the contents of their sacred book, they do treat it with reverence, almost to the point of idolatry.

God

According to Sikh belief there is one God who is absolute and sovereign over all things. Nanak's first statement after receiving his call became the opening sentences of the *Granth Sahib:*

> There is but one God, whose name is true, creator, devoid of fear and enmity, immortal, unborn, self-existent, great and bountiful. The True One was in the beginning (*Ibid.*, p. 35).

The usual name given to the Sikh deity is *"sat nam"* which means "true name," although god may be called many different names since He takes on various manifestations. The *Granth Sahib* records:

> Thou, O Lord, art One. But many are thy manifestations (*Ibid.*, p. 310).

Although God is basically a unity, according to Sikh doctrine, He is not considered personal but rather is equated with truth and reality. K. Singh observes:

> In equating God with the abstract principle of truth or reality, Nanak avoided the difficulty encountered by religious teachers who describe God only as the Creator of the Father...but Nanak's system has its own problems. If God is truth, what is truth? Nanak's answer was that in situations when you cannot decide for yourself, let the guru be your guide (K. singh in *Abingdon Dictionary of Living Religions*, Keith Grim, general editor, Nashville: Abingdon Press, 1981, p. 691).

Salvation

Robert E. Hume comments upon the Sikh idea of salvation:

> The Sikh religion teaches that salvation consists in knowing God, or in obtaining God, or being absorbed into God. The general method of salvation is fairly consistent with the supremacy of an inscrutable God, and with the accompanying doctrines of the worthlessness of the world and the helplessness of man...This method of obtaining salvation by a pantheistic merging of the individual self with the mystical world soul is identical with the method of

salvation which had been taught in the Hindu Upanishads" (Robert E. Hume, *The World's Living Religions*, New York: Charles Scribner's Sons, rev. ed., 1959, pp. 102, 103).

Hume lists the points of agreement and disagreement between Sikhism and the Hinduism and Islamic doctrines:

A COMPARISON OF SIKHISM WITH HINDUISM

(1) *Points of Agreement*

Theoretically, belief in a mystical Supreme Unity.

Practically, great variety of designations for deity.

A certain theistic application of pantheism, even as in some of the Hindu *Upanishads* and the *Bhagavad Gita*.

Salvation by faith in the grace of God.

The doctrine of Karma.

Transmigration of souls.

(2) *Points of Disagreement*

Hindu polytheism repudiated, in favor of a monistic pantheism.

Hindu pilgrimages, ritualism, and hermit asceticism repudiated, in favor of pure worship of the Pure One.

Hindu scriptures repudiated, in favor of the Sikh scriptures.

Hindu degradation of women repudiated, in favor of a higher regard for women.

Hindu infanticide repudiated, in favor of a more vigorous populating.

Hindu vegetarianism repudiated, in favor of a more vigorous meat-eating.

A COMPARISON OF SIKHISM WITH ISLAM

(1) *Points of Agreement*

Unity of the Supreme Personal Being.

Sovereignty of the Supreme Absolute Ruler.

A certain mercifulness attributed to the inscrutable deity, along with an uncomplainable arbitrariness.

Salvation through submission to God.

Worship through repetition of the name of the deity.

Great importance in repeating prescribed prayers.

Devotion to the founder as God's prophet.

Extreme reverence for sacred scripture.

The first section in the sacred scripture, a kind of Lord's Prayer, composed by the founder at a crisis in his early life when seeking for God, and subsequently prescribed for daily repetition by all his followers.

A series of subsequent leaders after the original founder.

A long, powerful, militaristic church state.

Unity among believers, despite subsequent sects.

A very important central shrine — Mecca and Amritsar.

Vehement denunciation of idolatry.

(2) *Points of Disagreement*

Sikhism's founder not so ruthless or violent as Islam's.

Sikhism's deity not so ruthless or violent as Islam's.

Sikhism's sacred scriptures ascribed to many teachers, at least thirty-seven; not to one, as in Islam.

No fasting prescribed to Sikhs, as to Muslims in month of Ramadan.

No decisive judgment-day in Sikhism, as in Islam. (*Ibid.*, pp. 108-110).

Sikhism and Christianity

The basic premise of Sikhism, uniting different religions, is foreign to the teachings of the Bible. Sikhism attempts to unify the contradictory faiths of Islam and Hinduism. Christianity teaches that it is the only true religion and demonstrates that its world view is consistent with reality.

Jesus Christ pointed out that those who do not believe in Him as their Savior will not receive everlasting life. "I said therefore to you, that you shall die in your sins; for unless you believe that I am He, you shall die in your sins" (John 8:24 NASB). "Jesus said to him, 'I am the way, and the truth, and the life; no one comes to the Father, but through Me'" (John 14:6 NASB).

The concept of God which Nanak obtained by uniting certain features from both Hinduism and Islam is abstract and impersonal, in contradistinction to the biblical concept of a personal, caring God.

The God who is revealed in the Bible is intimately involved with the actions of mankind. "O Lord, Thou hast searched me and known me. Thou dost know when I sit down and when I rise up. Thou dost understand my thought from afar. Thou dost scrutinize my path and my lying down, and art intimately acquainted with all my ways. Even before there is a word on my tongue, behold, O Lord, thou dost know it all" (Psalm 139:1-4 NASB).

The Bible makes it clear that Jehovah God cannot be reconciled with any other so-called god of another religion:

> "You are My witnesses," declares the Lord, "and My servant whom I have chosen, in order that you may know and believe Me, and understand that I am He. Before Me there was no God formed, and there will be none after Me" (Isaiah 43:10 NASB).

Sikhistic Terms

ANGAD—A disciple of Nanak who became the first in a line of ten successors as the leader of Sikhism. Angad introduced the teaching that Nanak was equal to God.

GRANTH SAHIB—The "Lord's Book." The sacred scripture of Sikhism.

GURU ARJAN—The compiler of the *Granth Sahib*, the sacred scripture of Sikhism.

MARDANA—The minstrel friend of Nanak who was his sole companion in the early years of the spreading of Sikhism.

NANAK—The 15th century A.D. religious leader who founded Sikhism.

SAT NAM—The "true name." This is the usual designation for God in Sikhism.

SIKH—Literally, "disciple." The designation for followers of Sikhism.

Sikhism Bibliography

Hume, Robert E., *The World's Living Religions*, New York: Charles Scribner's Sons, rev. ed., 1959.

McAuliffe, M. A., *Sikh Religion: Its Gurus, Sacred Writings, and Authors*, London: Oxford University Press, 1909.

Singh, K. in the *Abingdon Dictionary of Living Religions*, Keith Grim, general editor, Nashville: Abingdon Press, 1981.

A Christian Approach to Comparative Religions

Norman Anderson*

The study of comparative religion, fascinating though it is, leaves many with a sense of bewilderment. Such diverse beliefs are held by multitudes whose sincerity cannot be questioned that the student may easily fall into the logical absurdity of wondering whether any ultimate truth exists in matters of religion, or into the resigned pessimism of doubting whether any firmly founded conviction in such matters can be attained by man. Should not all religions be regarded, then as vain attempts to solve the insoluble or alternatively, as different roads, however devious, to one grand but distant goal? Admittedly, most of the world's faiths seem to the unprejudiced enquirer to be a patchwork of good and bad, or at least of the desirable and the less desirable; but cannot the mind which eschews fanaticism accept the postulate which seems in some sense common to all, that there is a Principle or a Person beyond and behind the material universe, which to recognize, or whom to worship, meets some craving of the human heart? As for the rest—the details of dogma and worship—may not each individual work out for himself an eclectic faith chosen from what seems best in all the great religions?

* From Sir Norman Anderson, ed., *The World's Religions*, Grand Rapids, MI: William B. Eerdmans Publishing Company, 1976. Used with permission from the publisher.

There are however, decisive reasons which preclude the Christian from adopting such an attitude. He will be vitally concerned, of course, with what millions of his fellow creatures believe, and their convictions will command not only his interest, but also his study and respect. More, he will find much in those who follow other religions which will rebuke, instruct and inspire him — as, for instance, the Muslim's fidelity in prayer and fast, the Buddhist's dignified self-discipline, and the Sadhu's detachment from the things of time and sense. But these things concern matters of observance rather than teaching, of practice rather than dogma, noble — and, in its context, valid — though much non-Christian dogma undoubtedly is. With the basic content of his faith, however, the Christian will neither want, nor dare, to meddle — although he will retain an insatiable longing to enter into a much deeper understanding of the revelation on which it rests and an ever richer experience of the God who thus reveals himself.

But how can the Christian be so confident that his faith does in fact rest on a uniquely authoritative self-revelation of God? The history of the Christian church is so darkened by the sin, intolerance, frailty and divisions of generations of its adherents that it is easy to understand the cynicism with which it is often regarded. Even the Christian religion, as it has been elaborated, expounded and embodied down the centuries, has been so fraught with human error that this, too, stands under the judgment of God. What is it, then, which gives the Christian his confident conviction in the essential truth and unique authority of the divine revelation which it is his duty and privilege to proclaim?

It is to Jesus himself that the Christian will continually return. Behind him, of course, stands the long history of Israel, and God's progressive revelation of himself through Abraham, Moses and a succession of prophets. But the Old Testament is always looking forward — whether through promise, prediction or prefiguration — to One who was to come. Then at last, as the apostle Paul puts it: 'When the time had fully come, God sent forth his Son, born of woman, born under the law, to redeem those who were under the law, so that we might receive adoption as sons' (Galatians 4:4, 5). And the whole New Testament bears witness to that unique event and its essential implications.

About the historicity of Jesus, about his basic teaching and the impact he made on his contemporaries, and about his death on a Roman gibbet, there can surely be no serious question. Nor is there any room for doubt that, after his death, something happened which transformed his little band of dejected and dispirited followers into a company of witnesses whom no persecution could silence, and who 'turned the world upside down.' One and all, moreover, they testified that what had happened was that the crucified Jesus had been raised from the dead and had appeared to them and many other witnesses. As Paul wrote to the Corinthians in a letter which is unquestionably authentic: 'I delivered to you first of all (or as a matter of first importance) what I also received, that Christ died for our sins in accordance with the scriptures, that he was buried, that he was raised on the third day in accordance with the scriptures, and that he appeared to Cephas, then to the twelve. Then he appeared to more than five hundred brethren at one time...' (1 Corinthians 15:3-5). Now Paul must himself have received this tradition, at least in outline, immediately after his own conversion, within between two and (at most) five years of the crucifixion; and he must certainly have received it in its fullness, with the appended list of the principal witnesses, on his first visit to Jerusalem (which he describes in the first chapter of his letter to the Galatians) just three years later. In all probability, then, he received it within five years of the alleged event. He tells us, moveover, that this was the common message of all the apostles (cf. 1 Corinthians 15:11). And he goes out of his way to assert that the majority of those five hundred witnesses to having seen the risen Christ were still alive when he wrote to the Corinthians some twenty years later. As C. H. Dodd put it: 'No statement could be more emphatic or unambiguous. In making it Paul is exposing himself to the criticism of resolute opponents who would have been ready to point to any flaw in his credentials or in his presentation of the common tradition.'[1] So the addition of

[1] C. H. Dodd, "The Appearances of the Risen Christ," in *Studies in the Gospels*, D. E. Nineham, ed., Naperville, IL: Allenson, 1955, p. 28.

this comment can only have meant: 'If you don't believe me, there are a very large number of witnesses still alive to whom you can turn for confirmation of what I say.'

It is perfectly true — as critics have not been slow to emphasize — that there is no explicit reference to the empty tomb in this earliest piece of historical evidence. But what oriental Jew of the first century could possibly have written that Christ died (physically, of course), that he was buried (physically, of course), and that he was later 'raised again on the third day' unless he had believed that *something* had happened to the body which had been laid in the sepulchre? When, from the very first, the early Christians — as C. H. Dodd again insists — said that 'He rose again from the dead,' they 'took it for granted that his body was no longer in the tomb. If the tomb had been visited it would have been found empty. The gospels supplemented this by saying, it *was* visited, it *was* found empty.'[2] And that this was an authentic part of the original apostolic tradition seems to me beyond any reasonable doubt.

But while it was the joyful certainty that Jesus was risen and still alive which was, unquestionably, the dominant note in the earliest apostolic proclamation, they soon began to put an equal emphasis on his atoning death. It was in the same letter to the Corinthians that Paul insisted that the gospel must be so preached that the cross of Christ should not 'be emptied of its power. For the word of the cross is folly to those who are perishing, but to us who are being saved it is the power of God' (1 Corinthians 1:17, 18). And in his second letter to the same church he explained this by saying, 'What I mean is, that God was in Christ reconciling the world to himself, no longer holding men's misdeeds against them, and that he has entrusted us with the message of reconciliation' (2 Corinthians 5:19, NEB). And the basis of this reconciliation was that, at the cross, God 'for our sake...made him to be sin who knew no sin, so that in him we might become the righteousness of God' (verse 21). This indeed, was the united testimony of the apostolic church, which they saw as the fulfilment

---

[2] C. H. Dodd, *The Founder of Christianity*, New York: MacMillan Company, 1970, p. 166.

of the fifty-third chapter of Isaiah and other Old Testament prophecies.[3]

It is for this reason that the Christian can allow no compromise, syncretism or theological relativism to obscure the inevitable intolerance — not in its spirit, but in its essential nature — of the gospel to which he is committed. It is not that he denies that there is any revelation of God's 'eternal power and Godhead' in the wonders of nature (*cf.* Romans 1 — 20) or in those glimpses of the truth which God has vouchsafed to many seeking souls. But if God could have *adequately* revealed himself in any other way, is it reasonable to suppose that he would have taken the almost incredible road to the incarnation and the passion? And if it had been possible to deal with the problem of man's sin and its consequences in any other way whatever, is it conceivable that God would not have 'spared his own Son' the physical, mental and spiritual agony of Calvary — an agony in which he himself was so intimately involved? Surely that would not make sense.

If, then, the basic Christian message is true — and for this the evidence seems wholly convincing — it must follow that, as Stephen Neill puts it:

'Simply as history the event of Jesus Christ is unique. Christian faith goes a great deal further in its interpretation of that event. It maintains that in Jesus the one thing that needed to happen has happened in such a way that it need never happen again... Making such claims, Christians are bound to affirm that all men need the Gospel. For the human sickness there is one specific remedy, and this is it. There is no other. Therefore the Gospel must be proclaimed to the ends of the earth and to the end of time. The Church cannot compromise on its missionary task without ceasing to be the Church. If it fails to see and to accept this responsilibity, it is changing the Gospel into something other than itself... Naturally, to the non-Christian hearer this must sound like crazy megalomania, and religious imperialism of the very worst kind. We must recognize the dangers; Christians have on many occasions fallen into both of them. But we are driven back ultimately on the question of truth.'[4]

---

[3] *Cf.* Mark 10:45; Luke 22:37; 1 Peter 2:24; *etc.*

[4] Stephen C. Neill, *Christian Faith and Other Faiths*, London: Oxford University Press, 1970, pp. 17f.

If many different groups of pathologists, let us suppose, were all seeking earnestly to discover the cause and cure of cancer, and one group — through no brilliance of their own — were to light upon the secret, would it constitute 'crazy megalomania' for them to share what they had found with their fellows? Would it not, rather, be criminal folly for them to keep the secret to themselves?

To what conclusion, then, does this lead us in regard to the attitude of the Christian to other religions as systems and to the eternal destiny of those who follow them? In regard to both these questions Christian opinion has been — and still is — widely divided. There have been many, all down the centuries, who have regarded most, if not all, of the non-Christian religions as a sort of *praeparatio evangelica* — as, indeed, all Christians would say of Old Testament Judaism. Some of those who take this view find the secret of the elements of truth in other religions in terms of an original divine revelation, the traces and influence of which have never been wholly lost or forgotten — or even in some cross-fertilization of ideas from one religion to another. Others, again, discern in them the influence of the 'cosmic Christ' who, as the eternal Logos or revealer of the Godhead, is the 'light that enlightens every man.' This view was taken by Justin Martyr and the Christian philosophers of Alexandria in the early centuries of the Christian era, and was summed up by William Temple when he wrote: 'By the word of God — that is to say by Jesus Christ — Isaiah and Plato, Zoroaster, Buddha, and Confucius uttered and wrote such truths as they declared. There is only one Divine Light, and every man in his own measure is enlightened by it.'[5]

Other Christians have adopted, at times, a diametrically opposite attitude. Instead of giving prominence to the elements of truth to be found in other religions they have emphasized the darker side of their ethical teaching and the less persuasive of their theological tenets, and have concluded that they emanate from the devil, rather than from God. In particular, those who take this view insist that these other religions clearly

---

[5]W. Temple, *Readings in St. John's Gospel*, New York: St. Martin's Press, 1945, I, p.10.

deny, whether by explicit statement or implicit teaching, the unique claims of the 'Word made flesh' and the fundamental need for the atonement that he alone could — and did — effect. Those elements of truth which can unquestionably be found in these other religions should therefore be explained, they feel, in terms of the fact that even Satan himself not infrequently appears as an angel of light — as, indeed, he might be expected to do in any religion designed to capture, and hold, men's allegiance and to constitute a substitute for, or an alternative to, the Christian gospel.

Yet a third view regards these other religions as not emanating primarily from either God or the devil, but as representing a variety of human attempts to explain the phenomena of life, to reach out after ultimate reality and to construct some system of thought, behaviour and religious observance which will satisfy man's needs. Those who founded and developed these religions were, like the rest of us, a compound of good and evil, of sincere aspiration after truth and of self-seeking; and they were also exposed to supernatural influences — both from God and Satan. It is scarcely to be wondered at, then that the non-Christian religions commonly represent such a diverse amalgam of truth and flasehood. All that is true must surely come from God, whether directly or indirectly; and all that is false must, presumably, owe its ultimate origin to the 'father of lies,' although its immediate source can usually be found in the sincere, but mistaken, conclusions of some human teacher.

The Christian preacher, then, will not feel that he can commend the non-Christian religions (other than Old Testament Judaism) as divinely inspired preparations for the gospel — although he will frequently, like the apostle Paul, use some element in their teaching or practice as a bridge by means of which he can reach the minds and hearts of their followers and bring to them the message he longs to communicate in an intelligible way. Nor will he — normally, at least — feel at liberty to speak against (or, still less, to ridicule) what other men sincerely, if mistakenly, believe, although he may at times be forced to speak out plainly about some particular point. His characteristic stance, however, will be positive rather than negative; and his habitual message will be to plead with all men to consider—or, in some cases, to reconsider—Jesus Christ. But far from any personal sense of superiority he will freely and frankly acknowledge that he is himself no better than anyone else; and he will do his best to present the essential Good News in a way which is stripped bare of accretions derived from the thought and culture of his own race or background. The truth as it is revealed in Jesus will be his one criterion, and the need of all men, without exception, for the forgiveness, reconciliation and new life which Jesus died to bestow will be the message he lives to proclaim.

But this means that he must listen quite as much as he speaks, for he needs to learn how someone from another religion and culture sees things. It is only then that the Christian 'may be given access to the dark places of that stranger's world—the things that really make him ashamed or anxious or despairing.' And then, at last, he will see the Saviour and Lord of that other world, his own Lord Jesus, yet not as he has known him hitherto. Instead he will 'understand how perfectly he matches all the needs and all the aspirations and all the insights of that other world—He who is the unique Lord and Saviour of all possible worlds.'[6] For every man, whatever his religion, race or moral virtue, is a sinner; and sin always and necessarily, alienates men from a holy God. So all of us alike need forgiveness, and all of us stand in need of a Saviour—since a sinful man can never save either himself or anyone else. It is precisely at this point, moreover, that the New Testament is at its most unequivocal, for Jesus himself is reported as saying, 'I am the way, and the truth, and the life; no one comes to the Father, but by me' (John 14:6)—or, in the Synoptic tradition, 'no one knows the Father except the Son and any one to whom the Son chooses to reveal him' (Matthew 11:27; cf. Luke 10:22). And the apostles in their turn reiterated this truth when they asserted that 'there is salvation in no one else, for there is no other name under heaven given among men by which we must be saved' (Acts 4:12).

---

[6] J.V. Taylor, *The Go-between God*, Philadelphia: Fortress Press, 1973, p. 189.

Inevitably, however, this raises in an acute form the question of the eternal destiny of those who, for example, have never so much as heard the truth as it is in Jesus. This is usually through no fault of their own, but rather through the failure of Christians to take sufficiently seriously the commission to preach the gospel to every creature. But if all men are sinners, and alike stand in need of forgiveness; if sinful men can never save either themselves or one another; and if there is only one Saviour—then what hope can any man have? Does this mean that they are inevitably lost? That would, indeed, be an agonizing conclusion to those whose basic belief is that 'God is love'; but is there really any alternative?

It is at this point, as I see it, that the Old Testament throws a ray of light on our darkness, for who can doubt that Abraham, Moses, David and a host of others enjoyed both forgiveness and fellowship with God? Yet they did not know Jesus and the salvation he was to effect—except as a vague hope of the future which they proclaimed but only dimly understood. And what of that multitude of more ordinary Jews who, convicted of sin by God's Spirit, turned to him in repentance and faith, brought the prescribed sacrifices, and threw themselves on his mercy? Were they not, too, forgiven and accepted—not because they had merited salvation, for no man can do this; nor on the basis of their animal sacrifices, which could never atone for human sin; but, rather, on the basis of what the God of love was going to do in the unique 'Lamb of God' who was still to come, and of that atoning death to which all the Old Testament sacrifices were designed to point. For this supreme event, although it certainly—and necessarily—happened at one particular time and place in human history, is timeless in its divine efficacy. And that this alone was the ultimate ground on which the transgressions and sins of Old Testament believers were forgiven seems to be clearly taught by New Testament verses such as Romans 3:25 and Hebrews 9:15.[7]

---

[7] There are also, of course, many verses which refer to the preincarnate Christ, through whom all things were created and in whom they are held together, whose atoning death was an essential part of the eternal counsel of God.

May this not provide us with a guideline to the solution of the burning problem of those in other religions who have never heard – or never heard with understanding – of the Saviour? It is not, of course, that they can earn salvation through their religious devotion or moral achievements, great though these sometimes are – for the New Testament is emphatic that no man can ever earn salvation. But what if the Spirit of God convicts them, as he alone can, of something of their sin and need; and what if he enables them, in the darkenss or twilight, somehow to cast themselves on the mercy of God and cry out, as it were, for his forgiveness and salvation? Will they not then be accepted and forgiven in the one and only Saviour? And if it be asked how this can be when they have never so much as heard of him, then the answer must be that they will be accepted on the basis of what the God of all grace himself did in Christ at the cross; for it is on that basis, alone, that a God who is light as well as love, just as well as merciful, can welcome and forgive repentant sinners.

It cannot be claimed that this is the clear and unequivocal teaching of the New Testament, where the primary emphasis is on the Christian's duty to share the Good News of God's love with the whole world. But how else can we understand Peter's words in the house of Cornelius: 'I now see how true it is that God has no favourites, but that in every nation the man who is godfearing and does what is right is acceptable to him' (Acts 10:34, 35, NEB)? This cannot mean that the man who does his best to be religious and moral will earn salvation, for the whole of the New Testament, as we have seen denies this possibility. But may it not mean that the man who realizes something of his need, and who casts himself on the mercy of God with a sincerity that shows itself in his life, will find that mercy where it is always available – at the cross where Jesus died?

If such a person should subsequently hear and understand the gospel, he would presumably be among the company of those (whom the Christian does meet, sometimes, in non-Christian lands) who accept it at once, and even say: 'Why didn't you come and tell me this before? It is what I have been waiting for all my life.' And if he never hears it in this life, then I believe he will wake up, as it were, on the other side of the grave to worship the One in whom, without understanding it, he had found the mercy of God.

This, it should be understood, is totally different from what has been termed the doctrine of the 'second chance'. In the latter it is the opportunity to choose, and the subsequent decision of faith, which are deferred to the after-life, while what I suggest happens to such a man beyond the grave is that he will come into the light of a joyful understanding of the salvation to which the Spirit of God has brought him through the repentance and faith which he inspired—faltering, it may be, and unenlightened, certainly—during the days of his earthly pilgrimage.

But if this is true—as I myself believe—then it certainly does not lessen the Christian's missionary responsibility. To begin with, his Master's last commission and command was that he should go and tell the Good News, and that should be quite enough. If, moreover, he reflects how he himself was brought to the point of no longer trying to earn salvation, but accepting it as a gift, he will almost certainly conclude that this was through hearing the gospel story and its implications; so how can he deny this privilege to others? Any who are enabled by the Holy Spirit to turn to God, in the twilight, in repentance and faith, would still, moreover, lack what assurance, conscious companionship and confident message which come only from a knowledge that Christ died to justify his people, rose again to manifest himself to them in the 'power of an endless life' and has commissioned them as his ambassadors to appeal to others to be reconciled to God. So it is our manifest duty to share this knowledge, and these privileges, with all mankind.

The question remains, however, whether the non-Christian religions may be said in any way to represent a 'saving structure which serves to point men to the cosmic Christ.' This is certainly the contention of Raymond Panikkar, who believes that the 'good and *bona fide* Hindu is saved by Christ and not by Hinduism, but it is through the sacraments of Hinduism, through the message of morality and the good life, through the mysterion that comes down to him through Hinduism, that Christ saves the Hindu normally.'[8] Somewhat similarly, W. Cantwell

Smith, writing of more than one non-Christian religion in the light of fellowship with their adherents, insists that we must recognize these religions as 'channels through which God Himself comes into touch with these His children.'[9] But it seems to me that both Panikkar and Cantwell Smith here go much too far. It is not through other religions as 'saving structures', as I see it, but rather through the basic fact of God's general revelation, vouchsafed in nature and in all that is true (including, of course, the truth there is in other religions), and the equally fundamental fact of our common humanity, that the Spirit of God, or the 'cosmic Christ', brings home to men and women something of their need. It is this, I think, which helps to explain what Lesslie Newbigin terms an 'element of continuity' which is 'confirmed in the experience of many who have become converts to Christianity from other religions. Even though this conversion involves a radical discontinuity, yet there is often the strong conviction afterwards that it was the living and true God who was dealing with them in the days of their pre-Christian wrestlings.'[10] This is naturally most clearly marked in Judaism, as in the case of the apostle Paul;[11] but I have also found that converts from Islam never regard the God whom they previously sought to worship as wholly false, but rather rejoice that they have now, in Jesus Christ, been brought to know, and have fellowship with, that God as he really is.

So, indeed, it is to Jesus Christ that we always, and inevitably, come back. 'A most sensitive, lonely man from Pakistan', John V. Taylor tells us, 'spoke at the New Delhi Assembly of the World Council of Churches about his conversion from Islam. All his longing was still for his own people, their language, their ancient culture; and in the factious and generally defeated church of that land he

---

[8]R. Panikkar, *The Unknown Christ of Hinduism*, New York: Humanities, 1968, p. 54.

[9]W. Cantwell Smith, *The Faith of Other Men*, New York: New American Library, 1963, p. 124.

[10]L. Newbigin, *The Finality of Christ*, Richmond, VA: John Knox Press, 1969, p. 59.

[11]*Cf.* Acts 22:3f., 14f.; 24:14f.; Galatians 1:15f., *etc.*

finds little consolation or fellowship. "I am a Christian," he confessed, "for one reason only—because of the absolute worship-ability of Jesus Christ. By that word I mean that I have found no other being in the universe who compels my adoration as he has done. And if ever some pundit or theologian should prove me wrong and show that, after all, the High God is not of the character which I see in Jesus, I, for one would have to blaspheme and turn my back on any such god."[12]

The attitude of the Christian, then, is essentially that of positive, humble, but unashamed witness to Jesus. As Lesslie Newbigin puts it, he

'points to the one Lord Jesus Christ as the Lord of all men... The Church does not apologise for the fact that it wants all men to know Jesus Christ and to follow him. Its very calling is to proclaim the Gospel to the ends of the earth. It cannot make any restrictions in this respect. Whether people have a high, a low or a primitive religion, whether they have sublime ideals or a defective morality makes no fundamental difference in this respect. All must hear the Gospel.'[13]

---

[12]Taylor, *op. cit.*, p. 193

[13]Newbigin, *op. cit.*, p. 59.

For Further Reading

Agency for Cultural Affairs. *Japanese Religions: A Survey by the Agency for Cultural Affairs.* Tokyo, Japan: Kodansha International, Ltd., 1972 and 1981.
   A non-Christian book concentrating on Buddhism but covering all the religions in Japan.

Anderson, Sir Norman, ed. *The World's Religions.* Grand Rapids, MI: William B. Eerdmans Publishing Co., 1975.
   A Christian book discussing religions of Pre-literary societies; Judaism; Buddhism; Islam; Hinduism; Shintoism; Confucianism; and concluding with a Christian approach to comparative religions.

Azzam, Abd-Al-Rahman. *The Eternal Message of Muhammad.* New York: The New American Library, 1964.
   A non-Christian book tracing some of the history of Islam.

Boa, Kenneth. *Cults, World Religions, and You.* Wheaton, IL: Victor Books, 1977.
   A Christian book covering major non-Christian religions of the East, major pseudo-Christian religions of the West, occult religions and systems, new religions and cults. Contains a good bibliography.

Burks, Thompson. *Religions of the World.* Cincinnati, OH: Standard Publishing Co., 1972.
   A Christian book designed for use as an adult education

course in Sunday school. Covers Judaism, Islam, Hinduism, and Christianity.

Chang, Lit-Sen. *Zen-Existentialism: The Spiritual Decline of the West.* Nutley, NJ: Presbyterian and Reformed Publishing Co., 1969.

Christian, probably the most in-depth view on Zen-Buddhism, especially as to how it affects American thought today.

Drummond, Richard. *Gautama the Buddha, An Essay in Religious Understanding.* Grand Rapids, MI: William B. Eerdmans Publishing Co., 1974.

Discusses the life of Buddha and his teachings. Includes theological interpretations and a Christian criticism.

Eastman, Roger, ed. *The Ways of Religion.* San Francisco, CA: Harper & Row Publishers, Inc., 1975.

An anthology in comparative religions combining pertinent and interesting primary sources and expository materials. College textbook, non-Christian.

Hesselgrave, David, J., ed. *Dynamic Religious Movements.* Grand Rapids, MI: Baker Book House, 1978.

Covers world religions in Africa, Europe, the Far East, the Middle East, North America, South America and Southeast Asia. A Christian book.

Heydt, Henry J. *A Comparison of World Religions.* Fort Washington, PA: Christian Literature Crusade, 1967.

Designed for use in a Sunday school or Bible class. A Christian book with good Christian perspectives. Historical survey of Judaism, Christianity, Hinduism, Zoroastrianism, Shintoism, Taoism, Jainism, Buddhism, Confucianism, Islam, and Sikhism, with a discussion of the sacred literature of each. Includes a topical comparison of the religions plus the distinctives of Christianity.

Marsh, C. R. *Share Your Faith with a Muslim.* Chicago, IL: Moody Press, 1975.

Contains the history of Islam, the five pillars of Islamic faith, Islamic teachings on essential Christian doctrines, and Christian answers to them.

Martin, Walter, ed. *The New Cults.* Santa Ana, CA: Vision House Publishers, Inc., 1980.

Although this deals mostly with new cults such as the Unification Church and Transcendental Meditation, it also contains information on Hinduism and Nichiren Shoshu Buddhism. A Christian book.

Miller, William McElwee. *The Baha'i Faith: Its History and Teachings.* Pasadena, CA: William Carey Library, 1974.

The most comprehensive, thorough and excellent treatment of Baha'ism available anywhere, written by a man who was a Christian missionary in Iran for over 40 years.

––––––––––––––. *A Christian Response to Islam.* Nutley, NJ: Presbyterian and Reformed Publishing Co., 1976.

This is the best single small book on a Christian approach to Islam. Contains the history of Islam, beliefs and practices of Muslims, and differences between Islam and Christianity. Gives testimonies of people converted from Islam, tips for presenting the Gospel to Muslims, and an excellent bibliography.

––––––––––––––. *Ten Muslims Meet Christ.* Grand Rapids, MI: William B. Eerdmans Publishing Co., 1969.

Testimonies of Muslims who came to Christ and who are from Islamic countries.

Needleman, Jacob. *The New Religions.* New York: E. P. Dutton, 1970.

A non-Christian book. Discusses some of the traditional world religions, as well as some new religions including the new American forms of Zen-Buddhism, Meher Baba, Subud, Transcendental Meditation, Krishna Murdi, Tibetan ideas in America, etc.

Neil, William, ed. *Concise Dictionary of Religious Quotations.* Grand Rapids, MI: William B. Eerdmans Publishing Co., 1974.

List of quotations by subject. Has a source index and subject index.

Palmer, Bernard. *Understanding the Islamic Explosion.* Beaver Lodge, Alberta, Canada: Horizon House Publishers, 1980.

Discusses contemporary Islam; the positions of women in Islamic tradition; the Koran versus the Bible; the prophet Mohammed; and the roots of Islam. Includes tips for sharing Christ with a Muslim.

Parrinder, Geoffrey. *A Dictionary of Non-Christian Religions.* Philadelphia, PA: The Westminster Press, 1971.

A comprehensive dictionary of the major terms of all the major religions. Good detail in a short space. Written from a Christian perspective but does not include Christianity as a world religion.

Pickthall, Mohammed Marmaduke, trans. *The Meaning of the Glorious Koran.* New York: New American Library, 1959.

Not a Christian book but an expository translation of the Koran. Since Islam teaches that the Koran is perfect and holy in Arabic, there is no authorized translation, but this is a good popular work.

Richardson, Don. *Eternity in Their Hearts.* Ventura, CA: Gospel Light Publications, 1981.

Written from a Christian perspective on the development of primitive religions. Though not very well documented, it does contain some good ideas.

Ridenour, Fritz. *So What's the Difference?* Ventura, CA: Gospel Light Publications, 1967 and 1979.

Deals with world religions and written from a Christian perspective. Includes Roman Catholicism; the major religions of the world: Judaism, Islam, Hinduism, Buddhism; and major cults: Unitarianism, Jehovah's Witnesses, Christian Science, and Mormonism. A pocket book, a little outdated, but contains good information.

Ringgren, Helmer. *Religions of the Ancient Near East.* Philadelphia, PA: The Westminster Press, 1973.

Covers Samarian religions, Babylonian and Assyrian religions, and West Semitic Religions. Deals with the major beliefs of those systems.

Jackson, Samuel Macauley, editor-in-chief. *The New Schaff-Herzog Encyclopedia of Religious Knowledge,* 15 volumes. Grand Rapids, MI: Baker Book House, updated in 1955.

Written from a Christian standpoint, though not always conservative. Covers all major issues in religious knowledge and world religions. A standard reference work, essential for serious study of religion. See also new revised edition (1980).

Sharpe, Eric J. *50 Key Words in Comparative Religions.* London: Lutterworth Press, 1971.

Alphabetical listing of subjects such as: ancestor worship, animism, astrology, mystery, mysticism, myth, phenomenology of religion, shaman, sin, soul, spirit, syncretism, witchcraft and worship.

Smith, Huston. *The Religions of Man.* New York: Harper and Row Publishers, 1958.

A widely quoted classic. Not necessarily the most reliable or the most up-to-date, but one of the first thorough treatments of Hinduism, Buddhism, Confucianism, Taoism, Islam, Judaism and Christianity.

Steinberg, Milton. *Basic Judaism.* New York: Harcourt Brace Jovanovich, Inc., 1975.

Excellent overview of general Judaism. Written from a Jewish perspective, covers the Torah, God, the good life, Israel and the nations, practices, law, institutions, and the world to come. Does not necessarily distinguish between the three major branches of Judaism.

Sumrall, Lester. *Where Was God When Pagan Religions Began?* Nashville, TN: Thomas Nelson Publishers, 1980.

Covers the cause and effect of pagan religions, animism, the religions of fear, Egyptian religion, a pattern for America, Babylonian religion, the roots of astrology, Hinduism, Buddhism, Shintoism, Confucianism, Taoism, Islam and end-time paganism. Written from a Christian perspective.

Tanenbaum, Marc H., Marvin Wilson and A. James Rudin, eds. *Evangelicals and Jews in Conversation.* Grand Rapids, MI: Baker Book House, 1978.

Divided into seven parts in which evangelical Christians and Jews share perspectives on the Messiah, Israel, interpretation of Scripture, response to moral crises and social problems, religious pluralism and the future.

An excellent source book on the differences between Judaism and Christianity and how Jews interact with Christians.

Vos, Johannes G. *A Christian Introduction to Religions of the World*. Grand Rapids, MI: Baker Book House, 1965.

A fairly old book and somewhat out of date, but a good, brief, and simple introduction to the major world religions, written from a Christian perspective.

Have You Heard of the
Four Spiritual Laws?

1

Just as there are physical laws that govern the physical universe, so are there spiritual laws which govern your relationship with God.

LAW ONE

GOD **LOVES** YOU, AND OFFERS A WONDERFUL **PLAN** FOR YOUR LIFE.

(References contained in this booklet should be read in context from the Bible wherever possible.)

Written by Bill Bright. Copyright © Campus Crusade for Christ, Inc., 1965. All rights reserved.

God's Love

"For God so loved the world, that He gave His only begotten Son, that whoever believes in Him should not perish, but have eternal life" (John 3:16).

God's Plan

(Christ speaking) "I came that they might have life, and might have it abundantly" (that it might be full and meaningful) (John 10:10).

Why is it that most people are not experiencing the abundant life?

Because . . .

LAW TWO

MAN IS SINFUL AND SEPARATED FROM GOD. THEREFORE, HE CANNOT KNOW AND EXPERIENCE GOD'S LOVE AND PLAN FOR HIS LIFE.

Man Is Sinful

"For all have sinned and fall short of the glory of God" (Romans 3:23).

Man was created to have fellowship with God; but, because of his stubborn self-will, he chose to go his own independent way and fellowship with God was broken. This self-will, characterized by an attitude of active rebellion or passive indifference, is evidence of what the Bible calls sin.

Man Is Separated

"For the wages of sin is death" (spiritual separation from God) (Romans 6:23).

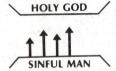

This diagram illustrates that God is holy and man is sinful. A great gulf separates the two. The arrows illustrate that man is continually trying to reach God and the abundant life through his own efforts, such as a good life, philosophy or religion.

The third law explains the only way to bridge this gulf . . .

LAW THREE

JESUS CHRIST IS GOD'S ONLY PROVISION FOR MAN'S SIN. THROUGH HIM YOU CAN KNOW AND EXPERIENCE GOD'S LOVE AND PLAN FOR YOUR LIFE.

He Died in Our Place

"But God demonstrates His own love toward us, in that while we were yet sinners, Christ died for us" (Romans 5:8).

He Rose from the Dead

"Christ died for our sins . . . He was buried . . . He was raised on the third day, according to the Scriptures . . . He appeared to Peter, then to the twelve. After that He appeared to more than five hundred . . ." (I Corinthians 15:3-6).

He Is the Only Way to God

"Jesus said to him, 'I am the way, and the truth, and the life; no one comes to the Father, but through Me' " (John 14:6).

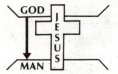

This diagram illustrates that God has bridged the gulf which separates us from Him by sending His Son, Jesus Christ, to die on the cross in our place to pay the penalty for our sins.

It is not enough just to know these three laws . . .

LAW FOUR

WE MUST INDIVIDUALLY **RECEIVE** JESUS CHRIST AS SAVIOR AND LORD; THEN WE CAN KNOW AND EXPERIENCE GOD'S LOVE AND PLAN FOR OUR LIVES.

We Must Receive Christ

"But as many as received Him, to them He gave the right to become children of God, even to those who believe in His name" (John 1:12).

We Receive Christ Through Faith

"For by grace you have been saved through faith; and that not of yourselves, it is the gift of God; not as a result of works, that no one should boast" (Ephesians 2:8,9).

When We Receive Christ, We Experience a New Birth.

(Read John 3:1-8.)

We Receive Christ by Personal Invitation

(Christ is speaking): "Behold, I stand at the door and knock; if any one hears My voice and opens the door, I will come in to him" (Revelation 3:20).

Receiving Christ involves turning to God from self (repentance) and trusting Christ to come into our lives to forgive our sins and to make us the kind of people He wants us to be. Just to agree intellectually that Jesus Christ is the Son of God and that He died on the cross for our sins is not enough. Nor is it enough to have an emotional experience. We receive Jesus Christ by faith, as an act of the will.

These two circles represent two kinds of lives:

SELF-DIRECTED LIFE
S — Self is on the throne
† — Christ is outside the life
• — Interests are directed by self, often resulting in discord and frustration

CHRIST-DIRECTED LIFE
† — Christ is in the life and on the throne
S — Self is yielding to Christ
• — Interests are directed by Christ, resulting in harmony with God's plan

Which circle best represents your life?
Which circle would you like to have represent your life?

The following explains how you can receive Christ:

YOU CAN RECEIVE CHRIST RIGHT NOW BY FAITH THROUGH PRAYER

(Prayer is talking with God)

God knows your heart and is not so concerned with your words as He is with the attitude of your heart. The following is a suggested prayer:

"Lord Jesus, I need You. Thank You for dying on the cross for my sins. I open the door of my life and receive You as my Savior and Lord. Thank You for forgiving my sins and giving me eternal life. Take control of the throne of my life. Make me the kind of person You want me to be."

Does this prayer express the desire of your heart?

If it does, pray this prayer right now, and Christ will come into your life, as He promised.

How to Know That Christ Is in Your Life

Did you receive Christ into your life? According to His promise in Revelation 3:20, where is Christ right now in relation to you? Christ said that He would come into your life. Would He mislead you? On what authority do you know that God has answered your prayer? (The trustworthiness of God Himself and His Word.)

The Bible Promises Eternal Life to All Who Receive Christ

"And the witness is this, that God has given us eternal life, and this life is in His Son. He who has the Son has the life; he who does not have the Son of God does not have the life. These things I have written to you who believe in the name of the Son of God, in order that you may know that you have eternal life" (I John 5:11-13).

Thank God often that Christ is in your life and that He will never leave you (Hebrews 13:5). You can know on the basis of His promise that Christ lives in you and that you have eternal life, from the very moment you invite Him in. He will not deceive you.

An important reminder . . .

DO NOT DEPEND UPON FEELINGS

The promise of God's Word, the Bible — not our feelings — is our authority. The Christian lives by faith (trust) in the trustworthiness of God Himself and His Word. This train diagram illustrates the relationship between **fact** (God and His Word), **faith** (our trust in God and His Word), and **feeling** (the result of our faith and obedience) (John 14:21).

FACT | FAITH | FEELING

The train will run with or without the caboose. However, it would be useless to attempt to pull the train by the caboose. In the same way, we, as Christians, do not depend on feelings or emotions, but we place our faith (trust) in the trustworthiness of God and the promises of His Word.

NOW THAT YOU HAVE RECEIVED CHRIST

The moment that you received Christ by faith, as an act of the will, many things happened, including the following:

1. Christ came into your life (Revelation 3:20 and Colossians 1:27).
2. Your sins were forgiven (Colossians 1:14).
3. You became a child of God (John 1:12).
4. You received eternal life (John 5:24).
5. You began the great adventure for which God created you (John 10:10; II Corinthians 5:17 and I Thessalonians 5:18).

Can you think of anything more wonderful that could happen to you than receiving Christ? Would you like to thank God in prayer right now for what He has done for you? By thanking God, you demonstrate your faith.

To enjoy your new life to the fullest . . .

SUGGESTIONS FOR CHRISTIAN GROWTH

Spiritual growth results from trusting Jesus Christ. "The righteous man shall live by faith" (Galatians 3:11). A life of faith will enable you to trust God increasingly with every detail of your life, and to practice the following:

G	Go to God in prayer daily (John 15:7).
R	Read God's Word daily (Acts 17:11)—begin with the Gospel of John.
O	Obey God moment by moment (John 14:21).
W	Witness for Christ by your life and words (Matthew 4:19; John 15:8).
T	Trust God for every detail of your life (I Peter 5:7).
H	Holy Spirit—allow Him to control and empower your daily life and witness (Galatians 5:16,17; Acts 1:8).

FELLOWSHIP IN A GOOD CHURCH

God's Word admonishes us not to forsake "the assembling of ourselves together. . ." (Hebrews 10:25). Several logs burn brightly together; but put one aside on the cold hearth and the fire goes out. So it is with your relationship to other Christians. If you do not belong to a church, do not wait to be invited. Take the initiative; call the pastor of a nearby church where Christ is honored and His Word is preached. Start this week, and make plans to attend regularly.

SPECIAL MATERIALS ARE AVAILABLE FOR CHRISTIAN GROWTH.

If you have come to know Christ personally through this presentation of the gospel, write for a free booklet especially written to assist you in your Christian growth.

A special Bible study series and an abundance of other helpful materials for Christian growth are also available. For additional information, please write Campus Crusade for Christ International, San Bernardino, CA 92414.

You will want to share this important discovery . . .